MW00609181

The
Affirming Flame

The
Affirming Flame

A POETICS OF
MEANING

Maurice S. Friedman

Prometheus Books
59 John Glenn Drive
Amherst, New York 14228-2197

Published 1999 by Prometheus Books

The Affirming Flame: A Poetics of Meaning.
Copyright © 1999 by Maurice S. Friedman.

Inquiries should be addressed to
Prometheus Books
59 John Glenn Drive, Amherst, New York 14228–2197
716–691–0133, ext. 207. FAX: 716–564–2711.
WWW.PROMETHEUSBOOKS.COM

03 02 01 00 99   5 4 3 2 1

Library of Congress Cataloging-in-Publication Data

Friedman, Maurice S.
    The affirming flame : a poetics of meaning / Maurice S. Friedman.
        p.   cm.
    Includes bibliographical references.
    ISBN 1–57392–259–5 (alk. paper)
    1. Literature, Modern—History and criticism. 2. Meaning (Philosophy) in
literature. I. Title.
PN49.F665   1999
809′.93384—dc21   98–47271
                                                                          CIP

Printed in the United States of America on acid-free paper

PN
49
.F665
1999

To the Memory of
Milton O. Percival
Teacher and Friend

We must take unto ourselves the problematic of modern man and shape from it an image of meaningful human existence; an image that neither leaves out this problematic nor simply reflects it but wrestles with it, contends with it until it has found a way forward. Our foremost task is to mold the resistant clay of contradiction and absurdity into a figure of genuine humanity.

Maurice Friedman, *The Hidden Human Image*

Contents

Part I—Finding Meaning in the Lived Concrete

7

CONTENTS

Contents

Part III—Holding the Tension between Affirming and Withstanding

Acknowledgments

The author acknowledges the kind permission of authors and publishers who have enabled him to reprint literary selections included in this book.

1. Emily Dickinson, poems 76, 184, 185, 258, 301, 313, 338, 341, 377, 476, 886, 976, 1129, 1413. Reprinted by permission of the publishers and trustees of Amherst College from *The Poems of Emily Dickinson*, Thomas H. Johnson, ed., Cambridge, Mass.: The Bellknap Press of Harvard University Press, copyright © 1951, 1955, 1979, 1983 by the President and Fellows of Harvard College.

2. Yehuda Amichai, selections from *Travels: A Bilingual Edition*, trans. from the Hebrew by Ruth Nevo (New York: The Sheep Meadow Press, 1986). Reprinted with permission from The Sheep Meadow Press, New York.

3. Yehuda Amichai, selections from *The Selected Poetry of Yehuda Amichai*, ed. and newly trans. by Chana Bloch and Steven Mitchell (New York: Harper & Row, 1986). Copyright © 1996 The Regents of the University of California. Reprinted by permission.

4. Rainer Maria Rilke, selections from *Duino Elegies*, trans. by J. B. Leishman and Stephen Spender (New York: W. W. Norton, 1939). Translation copyright © 1939 by W. W. Norton & Company, Inc., renewed © 1967 by Stephen Spender and J. B. Leishman. Reprinted by permission of W. W. Norton & Company, Inc. (USA) and St. John's College Oxford and The Hogarth Press (UK).

5. Pablo Neruda, "Gautama Christ," from *Winter Garden*, trans. by William O'Daly (P.O. Box 271, Port Townsend, Wash.: Copper Canyon Press, 1986). Copyright © 1986 by Pablo Neruda, translated by William O'Daly. Reprinted by permission of Copper Canyon Press.

6. Czeslaw Milosz, "How It Was," "From the Rising of the Sun: Diary of a Naturalist," from *Bells in Winter*, trans. by the author and Lillian Vallee (Manchester, England: Carcanet New Press Ltd., 1982). Copyright © 1974, 1977, 1978 by Czeslaw Milosz. Reprinted by permission of The Ecco Press.

7. Czeslaw Milosz, "Meditation," "On a Beach," "Inheritor," "Meaning," from *Provinces*, trans. by the author and Robert Hass (New York: The Ecco Press, 1991). Copyright © 1991 by Czeslaw Milosz Royalties, Inc. Reprinted by permission of The Ecco Press and Sterling Lord Literistic, Inc.

8. W. B. Yeats, selections from *The Collected Works of W. B. Yeats*, vol. I: *The Poems*, rev. ed. (New York: Macmillan, 1956).

"Circus Animals' Desertion." Reprinted with the permission of Scribners, a Division of Simon & Schuster from *The Collected Works of W.B. Yeats*, vol. I: *The Poems*, revised and edited by Richard J. Finneran. Copyright © 1940 by Georgie Yeats; copyright renewed © 1968 by Bertha Georgie Yeats, Michael Butler Yeats, and Anne Yeats; and by A. P. Watts Ltd. on behalf of Michael B. Yeats.

Stanza IV from "Vacillation" and excerpt from "Crazy Jane Talks with the Bishop." Reprinted with the permission of Scribner, a Division of Simon & Schuster from *The Collected Works of W. B. Yeats*, vol. I: *The Poems*, revised and edited by Richard J. Finneran. Copyright © 1933 by Macmillan Publishing Company; copyright renewed © 1961 by Bertha Georgie Yeats; and by A. P. Watts Ltd. on behalf of Michael B. Yeats.

"Sailing to Byzantium" (excerpt). Reprinted with the permisison of Scribner, a Division of Simon & Schuster from *The Collected Works of W. B. Yeats*, vol. I: *The Poems*, revised and edited by Richard J. Finneran. Copyright © 1928 by Macmillan Publishing Company; copyright renewed © 1956 by Georgie Yeats; and by A. P. Watts Ltd. on behalf of Michael B. Yeats.

"The Second Coming" (selections). Reprinted with the permission of Scribner, a Division of Simon & Schuster from *The Collected Work of W. B. Yeats*, vol. I: *The Poems*, revised and edited by Richard J. Finneran. Copyright © 1924 by Macmillan Publishing Company, renewed © 1952 by Bertha Georgie Yeats; and by A. P. Watts Ltd. on behalf of Michael B. Yeats.

9. Denise Levertov, "The Showings: Lady Julian of Norwich, 1342–1416," "Variation and Reflection on a Theme by Rilke," from *Breathing the Water* (New York: New Directions Publishing Corporation, 1987). Copyright © 1987 by Denise Levertov. Reprinted by permission of New Directions Publishing Corporation, Laurence Pollinger Limited, and the estate of Denise Levertov.

10. Denise Levertov, "The Avowal," "Oblique Prayer," "The Task," ". . . That Passeth All Understanding," "Of Being," "Passage," from *Oblique Prayers. New Poems with 14 Translations from Jean Joubert* (New York: New Directions Publishing Corporation, 1985). Copyright © 1984 by Denise Levertov. Reprinted by permission of New Directions Publishing Corporation, Laurence Pollinger Limited, and the estate of Denise Levertov.

11. Denise Levertov, "The Depths," "Come into Animal Presence," from *Denise Levertov: Poems 1960–1967* (New York: New

ACKNOWLEDGMENTS

Directions Publishing Corporation, 1983). Copyright © 1966 by Denise Levertov. Reprinted by permission of New Directions Publishing Corporation, Laurence Pollinger Limited, and the estate of Denise Levertov.

12. Denise Levertov, "Intimation," "El Salvador: Requiem and Invocation," "In California: Morning, Evening, Late January," "The Love of Morning," from *A Door in the Hive* (New York: New Directions Publishing Corporation, 1989). Copyright © 1989 by Denise Levertov. Reprinted by permission of New Directions Publishing Corporation, Laurence Pollinger Limited, and the estate of Denise Levertov.

14. Dylan Thomas, selections from "Poem on His Birthday," from *The Collected Poems of Dylan Thomas, 1934–1952* (New York: New Directions Publishing Corporation, 1971). Copyright ©1952 by Dylan Thomas. Reprinted by permission of New Directions Publishing Corporation and David Higham Associates Ltd.

15. W. H. Auden, "In Memory of W. B. Yeats," from *W. H. Auden: Collected Poems* by W. H. Auden, Copyright © 1940 and renewed 1968 by W. H. Auden. Reprinted by permission of Random House, Inc.

16. W. H. Auden, "Christmas 1940," from *W. H. Auden: Collected Poems* by W. H. Auden, Copyright © 1945 by W. H. Auden. Reprinted by permission of Random House, Inc.

17. W. H. Auden, "The Wanderer," from *W. H. Auden: Collected Poems* by W. H. Auden, Copyright © 1934 and renewed 1962 by W. H. Auden. Reprinted by permission of Random House, Inc.

18. W. H. Auden, "September 1, 1939," from *W. H. Auden: Collected Poems* by W. H. Auden, Copyright © 1940 by W. H. Auden. Reprinted by permission of Random House, Inc.

19. T. S. Eliot, "Dry Salvages," from *Four Quartets*, from *Collected Poems 1909–1962* (New York: Harcourt Brace & World,

14

Inc., 1971). Copyright © 1943 by T. S. Eliot and renewed 1971 by Esme Valerie Eliot, reprinted by permission of Harcourt Brace & Company (USA) and Faber and Faber (UK).

20. Nellie Sachs, "O the Chimneys," "But Who Emptied Your Shoes of Sand," "Even the Old Man's Last Breath," "What Secret Cravings of the Blood," "You Onlookers," "I Do Not Know the Room," "Glowing Enigmas," from *O the Chimneys: Selected Poems, Including the Verse Play, ELI*, translated from the German by Michael Hamburger, Christopher Holmes, Ruth and Matthew Mead, and Michael Roloff (New York: Farrar, Straus & Giroux, 1967). © Surhkamp Verlag Frankfurt am Main 1961. Translation copyright © 1967 and copyright renewed © 1995 by Farrar, Straus & Giroux, Inc.

21. Pablo Neruda, "With Her," "Not Quite So Tall," "Point," from *Extravagaria*, a bilingual edition, trans. by Alastair Reid (New York: Farrar, Straus & Giroux, 1974). Translation copyright © 1974 by Alastair Reid.

22. Pablo Neruda, "The Poet's Obligation," "Fully Empowered," "To the Dead Poor Man," from *Fully Empowered*, trans. by Alastair Reid (New York: Farrar, Straus & Giroux, 1975). Translation copyright © 1975 by Alastair Reid.

23. Theodore Roethke, "In a Dark Time," from *The Collected Poems of Theodore Roethke* (New York: Doubleday, 1960). Copyright © 1960 by Beatrice Roethke, Administratrix of the Estate of Theodore Roethke. Used by permission of Doubleday, a division of Bantam Doubleday Dell Publishing Group, Inc. (USA) and Faber and Faber (UK).

24. Paul Celan, selections from *Poems of Paul Celan*, trans. and intro. by Michael Hamburger (London: Anvil Press Poetry, 1988). Reprinted by permission of Persea Books (USA) and Anvil Press Poetry Ltd. (UK).

25. Mikhail Bakhtin, selections from *Problems in Dostoevsky's Poetics* (Minneapolis: University of Minnesota Press, 1984). Reprinted by permission of University of Minnesota Press.

26. Steven Kepnes, selections from *The Text as Thou: Martin Buber's Dialogical Hermeneutics and Theological Narrative* (Bloomington: Indiana University Press, 1992). Reprinted by permission of Indiana University Press.

27. André Schwarz-Bart, selections from *The Last of the Just*, trans. by Stephen Becker (New York: Atheneum, Inc., 1960). Originally published in French as *Le dernier des justes*, by Editions du Seuil, Paris. Copyright © 1959 by Editions du Seuil. Reprinted by permission of Georges Borchardt, Inc.

Preface

This book is the continuation of an old and longstanding love: my dialogue with modern literature. The master's thesis that I wrote for my M.A. in English at Ohio State University in 1947 was devoted to ten European novels (not including English or American ones!). One of my earliest books was *Problematic Rebel*,[1] an intensive study of the writings of Melville, Dostoyevsky, Kafka, and Camus. Another was *To Deny Our Nothingness: Contemporary Images of Man*,[2] which contains, along with philosophy, psychology, and religion, studies of the writings of many literary figures: T. S. Eliot, André Gide, Georges Bernanos, Graham Greene, Carlo Coccioli, Aldous Huxley, Martin Buber, André Malraux, Nikos Kazantsakis, Hermann Hesse, Jean-Paul Sartre, Albert Camus, Samuel Beckett, Franz Kafka, and Elie Wiesel.

Although here and there, as with the sections on Melville's *Moby Dick* and Kafka's *The Castle*, I draw on my earlier books, *The Affirming Flame* is in no sense a summary of these works. Yet it is in another sense a continuation and a conclusion. At one point I was going to call the book itself "The Poetics of the Spirit," but then, persuaded that "spirit" is entirely too vague a term for the contemporary reader, I changed it to "A Poetics of Dialogue" and used it as the subtitle. Then at the last minute it struck me that, after all, "A Poetics of Meaning" is actually what the book is about, and I have used that as a subtitle instead.

Despite its demotion, I still want to say something about "a poetics of dialogue" since it gives a clue to the way in which I relate to literature. By "a poetics of dialogue" I mean the spirit as *between* used as an approach to literature and its interpretation. In so far as the literary stance of this book is that of "a poetics of dialogue," it is, of course, a product not only of almost half a century of concern with modern literature, but also of my concern with that philosophy of dialogue which I have expounded in many books in the language of Martin Buber and in my own. For the benefit of those readers who may be interested, I have added a hermeneutical appendix, "Toward a Poetics of Dialogue."

This book is an invitation to a dialogue with literature itself. For this reason it includes not only extensive discussion of many modern novels and poems but also extensive quotations from the literature itself. It is at the same time an invitation to bring into this dialogue with modern literature what might be thought of as a basically philosophical concern, though one that can only be grasped properly through the literature itself. This is the discovery of meaning through the meeting with the particular.

We are likely to find ourselves abandoned in the face of the threat of meaninglessness that comes with the shattering of security and the agony of doubt, and still more so when the meaning found through the meeting with the particular is destroyed by the encounter with evil. This threat of abandonment never totally disappears even when meaning is found in "Holding the Tension between Affirming and Withstanding," as I portray it in Part Three of this book.

This meaning is never that of a comfortable faith or a harmonic *Weltanschauung*. It is tragic at best and more often grotesque. In the *Shoah* (or Holocaust), which I call the "Ultimate Confrontation," it goes beyond anything with which we are familiar from our ordinary lives. It is, nonetheless, a meaning reached in dialogue, as opposed to that subjective affirmation of meaning *in spite of the absurd* affirmed by the Camus of *The Myth of Sisyphus* or the invention of values championed by Sartre.

In concluding this book with a chapter on "Confronting Death" I not only touch on the existential condition of every person who has ever lived. I also illuminate much of our modern and contemporary situation. In our time death itself has often become, in the words of the psychohistorian Robert Jay Lifton, "absurd death."

In focusing on death in the conclusion I am also focusing on one of the themes that arises most persistently and profoundly in great modern literature. That this is also an extension and application of my own philosophy in no way gainsays this book's central concern with modern literature. Indeed, I was able to write this chapter only by extensive quotations from a wide range of literature, including much that is dealt with in the body of this book.

I must once again express my gratitude to Eugenia Friedman, this time for her help with the poetry in this book. She has an inexhaustible knowledge and love of modern poetry that I have greatly profited from as well as from her specific reactions to the chapters on poetry that are included here. I am also indebted to my friend Linda Danton, reference librarian at the University of California San Diego, for her invaluable assistance in finding books for me. I am indebted, too, to Professor Kenneth Kramer and Dr. Pat Boni of the departments of religious studies at San Jose State and San Diego State Universities, respectively. Both are friends of many years who were students in the Ph.D. program in religion and literature that I founded and directed at Temple University in the late sixties and early seventies. Professor Kramer in particular has given me decisive help with the difficult task of revision—of bringing the book into clear focus so that it might attain its true form. My old friend Robert McAfee Brown gave me valuable suggestions at an early stage of this book, and he and another old friend, Elie Wiesel, wrote to their own editors to try to find a publisher for my book. My friend and former editor Richard Huett and my friend Virginia Shabatay have helped me reach the final stage of this book in which we hope it will appeal to the intelligent lay person. Richard Huett has also made many helpful suggestions for improving the text. Finally, I must thank my friend and one-time graduate student Dewey deButts for untold help in preparing the manuscript of this book at several different stages.

Maurice Friedman
Solana Beach, California
December 1998

Introduction

A Poetics of Meaning

The Search for Meaning

The heart of my dialogue with modern literature in this book is the search for meaning through the meeting with the particular. This search for meaning is integrally connected with the poetics of meeting that I shall elaborate in the hermeneutical appendix. It is not a search for a meaning that is already given "out there" any more than it is for a meaning that can be brought up out of the depths of the self. It is the search for a meaning that can only be reached by our wrestling all night with the angel, as Jacob did, and demanding of it a blessing. It is meaning of dialogue, understood not as two people talking but as mutuality, commitment, involvement, and presentness, *and* it is a meaning found throughout the meeting with the particular.

In his essay "Religion and Philosophy" Martin Buber asserts that "philosophy is grounded on the presupposition that one sees

21

the absolute in universals," whereas when religion has to define itself philosophically, it "says that it means the covenant of the absolute with the particular, with the concrete." Buber generalizes this statement into the assertion that the religious essence in every religion is its highest certainty—"the certainty that the meaning of existence is open and accessible in the actual lived concrete, not above the struggle with reality but in it." This does *not* mean that meaning is to be won through any type of analytical or synthetic investigation or reflection upon the lived concrete. "Meaning is to be experienced . . . in the unreduced immediacy of the moment," and this precludes aiming at experiencing the experience, for that destroys the spontaneity of the mystery:

> Only he reaches the meaning who stands firm, without holding back or reservation, before the whole might of reality and answers it in a living way. He is ready to confirm with his life the meaning which he has attained.[1]

If we cannot always assert that meaning is open and accessible in the "lived concrete," we can, nonetheless, abjure that philosophy and spirituality that rises above it to some "higher plane" in favor of searching for meaning in the particular itself. Like William James's pragmatism, we will count the humblest and most personal experiences, including the mystical, and "will take a God who lives in the very dirt of private fact—if that should seem a likely place to find Him."[2]

The search for meaning in the particular is inextricably interwoven into modern literature and our dialogue as it is into any conceivable poetics of meeting. The original title of Viktor Frankl's famous book *The Search for Meaning* was *From Death Camp to Existentialism.* Although Frankl would maintain, and we would agree, that human beings have always searched for meaning, it is precisely today when we have had to face the Holocaust and so many other historical realities that seem absurd by their very nature that this search has become most desperate and most acute.

Of the many literary figures that we might select to illustrate this search, none is more paradigmatic of the progression from the bond with the universal to the bond with the particular than Hermann Hesse. Hesse's novel *Siddartha* juxtaposes the spiritual pilgrimage of the young Brahmin Siddhartha with the figure of Sakyamuni, or the Buddha, who is also traditionally called Siddhartha. Hesse's Siddhartha evolves within himself a new teaching—not to escape from and destroy himself but to understand and learn from himself. Now the true Self is no longer identified with the Hindu Atman, the absolute Self, but with Siddhartha, a particular being, who lives separated and different from everybody else. "I will learn from myself the secret of Siddhartha," he says to himself. Instead of scorning diversity for unity he would find unity in diversity. "Meaning and reality were not hidden somewhere behind things, they were in them, in all of them." Instead of seeing the visible world as *maya,* or the veil of illusion, Siddhartha now looks at the world in a simple, childlike way, without seeking to penetrate to any reality behind it. Instead of trying to put aside the senses and trap his Self in a net of thoughts, as he had done before, he now recognizes that both senses and thoughts are fine things behind which "lay hidden the last meaning."

"It is hard to find [the] track of the divine," Harry exclaims in Hesse's next great novel, *Steppenwolf.* He pursues the fleeting, fluttering significance of his life over its ruins; even while he suffers its seeming meaninglessness and madness, he hopes "secretly at the last turn of Chaos for revelation and God's nearness." Not narrowing the world and simplifying the soul, but taking the whole world into his soul must be his way. The personality is not abolished, but lifted and enlarged; yet it is lifted through suffering. Man

23

is not a fixed and enduring form, but an experiment and a transition. "He is nothing else than the narrow and perilous bridge between nature and spirit," Haller asserts in the spirit of Nietzsche.

At the end of the novel, the easy division between the trivial outer world and the transcendent world of the immortals is no longer allowed Harry. Instead, he has to encounter life, reverence the spirit that manifests itself through it but cannot be identified with it, and laugh at the absurdities with which its music is cluttered and obscured.

The "call" that comes to Joseph Knecht, the hero of *Magister Ludi,* is an awakening of the soul, "so that inner dreams and premonitions are suddenly replaced by a summons from without." This is fitting since the name Knecht itself means servant in German. No longer is one's destiny seen as something that has already taken place within one, reflected only by outer events. Instead, these events themselves are a reality that calls the chosen ones to their vocation. Moreover, for Joseph Knecht, this event takes the form of an image of the human through *response* to which he becomes himself. This image of the human is embodied in the Magister Musicae, who shows Joseph, almost without words, what music really means and brings him to presentness by his own concentrated presence.

In the course of his activities as Magister Ludi, Joseph Knecht discovers the meaning that is to be found in direct relationship between person and person. He discovers the joy of teaching and of educating. This means the struggle "for an exact identification between person and office," and it means simultaneously "the joy that ensues from the transplanting of knowledge already gained into other minds and of seeing it take on completely new appearances and radiations." In the end Joseph Knecht leaves his high office and breaks with the Order to go out into the world in order to find "a simple natural task—a human being who has need of me." An "awakening," he now realizes, is "not so much a question of realizing truth"—gnosis—"but of experiencing reality and of sustaining it." Joseph Knecht's personal way is not the voice of the "inner man." It is the call of a reality that cannot be swallowed into his soul yet places a demand on it. Joseph Knecht's "awakenings" are not divine manifestations or absolute truth to him, but existential reality, "monstrously real in their presence and inescapability."

In "Hermann Hesse's Service to the Spirit," the speech that Martin Buber gave on the occasion of Hesse's eightieth birthday, Buber pointed to Hesse's discovery of the reality of the spirit in the "between"—in the life of events between person and person. "It is the reality of the spirit which builds worlds out of the world, and this spirit is in the final ground a communal one."

> The spirit . . . has collapsed into itself and has made war on itself, and since then it can no longer be for us a competent helper . . . it has betrayed us, for it was no longer a whole and united spirit . . . It can only become whole and united when it stakes itself for our unity.[3]

In this encomium Buber is undoubtedly referring to the terrible events that have marked the twentieth century: the two world wars, Nazism, the Holocaust, the atomic bomb, the "cold war" that followed it, the slave labor camps of the Gulag Archipelago, and not least the crisis of the Western world in which we take the "spiritual" with grim seriousness but allow it to have no binding claim on our lives. Hesse and Buber have pointed us beyond the search for meaning as an inner and individual self-realization to the discovery of the reality of the spirit in the "between." Through his commentary on Hesse's service to the spirit, moreover, Buber has pointed us to the common task of repairing the injured human order. We can only do this in our day through holding the tension between affirming and withstanding.

25

The Argument of this Book

In the first section we have already touched on two aspects of the Poetics of Meaning that informs this book. The first is the search for meaning itself and the second the fact that this search is conducted through a discussion of literature rather than through abstract philosophy or science. The third, which we shall spell out here, is the argument, or the progression of thought. A half century ago when I took a graduate course in literary theory at Ohio State University from Professor Milton Percival, I was struck by John Crowe Ransom's definition of a good poem as one that has the right balance between "vehicle" and "texture." By "vehicle" he means the progression of thought from stanza to stanza within the poem. By "texture" he means the imagery found in each stanza. This definition still seems valid to me, and not for poetry alone but also for a work such as Abraham Joshua Heschel's philosophy of religion *Man Is Not Alone*—a book so rich in poetic imagery that many readers cannot follow the highly cogent logical progression that it contains. A bad poem, according to Ransom, is one that has too much vehicle and too little imagery or, conversely, so much imagery that the vehicle is lost sight of. In *The Affirming Flame* the texture is not only the actual quotations from literature but the discussion of that literature in so far as it does not pertain to the movement of thought of the book as a whole. The movement of thought is, of course, the vehicle. It is my hope that I have presented the literature sufficiently sparsely and succinctly that it does not obscure the progression of the argument.

To make doubly sure that this is so, I wish to outline the argument itself here with the briefest indication of the literature which illustrates it. Only thus can it be philosophy through literature without reducing the literature to mere illustration or the philosophy to the empty framework of an anthology.

I see the argument, or progression of thought, as a clear movement from thesis to antithesis to synthesis in the precise sense in which Hegel used it. The thesis is the discovery of meaning in the particular, or the "lived concrete," as Buber puts it. The first chapter of Part One discusses briefly what I call the "mysticism of the particular" found in Taoist, Zen Buddhist, and Hasidic masters and a number of poetic mystics of the particular from the seventeenth century to the present: Thomas Traherne, William Blake, Walt Whitman, Dostoevsky's Father Zossima, Black Elk, and Abraham Joshua Heschel. Since our concern is not comparative mysticism, the second chapter in Part One is entitled "Poets of the Here and Now"—under which rubric I discuss the great German-speaking Czech poet Rainer Maria Rilke, and three contemporary poets, Denise Levertov, Annie Dillard, and Wendell Berry. In contrast to the last three Rilke's concern with the "here and now" extends only to nature and objects and not to his fellow human beings.

In Part Two—the antithesis—I discuss the threat of meaninglessness that must be confronted by those who have found meaning in their meeting with the particular only to see it eclipsed by evil and the absurd. I have divided Part Two into four chapters. The first is "The Shattering of Security," which I illustrate through Melville's *Moby Dick* and Achebe's *Things Fall Apart*. The second is "Faith, Anguish, and Doubt," powerfully embodied in Emily Dickinson, Gerard Manley Hopkins, and Denise Levertov. The third is "The Demonism of Nature," amply set forth in *Moby Dick*, and the fourth is "Human Demonism," illustrated through the inhumane treatment of the Native American, the African American, and the Jew.

When I put forward Part Three—"Holding the Tension between Affirming and Withstanding"—as the synthesis, I am not, of course, suggesting any return to the original wholeness and innocence of Part One. What I am saying, rather, is that it *is* possible to affirm—not despite evil and the absurd, as the early Camus would have it, but by bringing precisely these into our own dialogue with existence so that, with clear-sighted trust, we may, as I put it in my book *Problematic Rebel*, affirm where we can affirm and withstand where we must withstand. Just what can be affirmed and what must be withstood must be discovered anew in each situation. For this reason it seems to me necessary to have a variegated illustration of our "synthesis" through four different chapters. The first is a juxtaposition of Franz Kafka and Milan Kundera, whom I characterize as the modern and the postmodern absurd. The second chapter holds the tension between the harmonic, the tragic, and the grotesque as we find it in the poetry of W. B. Yeats, W. H. Auden, Pablo Neruda, and Czeslaw Milosz. The third is "The Scandal of the Particular," in which meaning in the particular is combined with the absurd—beautifully illustrated by the Israeli poet Yehuda Amichai, Denise Levertov, and Annie Dillard, to whom I owe the title of this chapter. The fourth is the *Shoah*, or Holocaust, as the "ultimate confrontation" which tests as nothing else can the assertion that meaning can be found even in the encounter with evil and the absurd. Here I discuss four quite different representatives of the literature of the Shoah (leaving out my old friend Elie Wiesel, to whom I have already devoted ten chapters of my 1987 book *Abraham Joshua Heschel and Elie Wiesel: "You Are My Witnesses"*): André Schwarz-Bart, Primo Levi (who was our illustration for "Human Demonism" in relation to the Jews), and Nellie Sachs and Paul Celan. The last two form one unit because of their personal and spiritual connection. If I devote much more space to Paul Celan than to Nellie Sachs, it is because he is for me paradigmatic of holding the tension between affirming and withstanding.

The Conclusion—"Confronting Death"—is an extension of Part Three in its application of the meaning found in the face of evil and the absurd to what is at once a universal phenomenon—death and the expectation of death—and the "absurd death" which our time has experienced as no other. I must repeat once again that this meaning is neither worldview nor theology. It is the meaning of the dialogue itself that in no way reduces or denies the evil and absurdity with which we have lived. This part of the book, too, has its fair share of literary illustrations—by too many authors to list—but these are set within the context of my own philosophy. In this chapter the "vehicle" is at least as prominent as the "texture," which hopefully will help the reader understand the thread of argument of the book as a whole.

Part One

Finding Meaning
in the Lived Concrete

1

Mystics of the Particular

The particularity and uniqueness that are implicit in the dialogue with literature that we take as our approach are
grounded in a phenomenon that is found in much religion and literature that far predates the modern. This phenomenon is a special type of mysticism which does not need to put aside the world
of the senses in order to find mystical realization. I call this the
"mysticism of the particular" (my own coinage[1]). Such mysticism
celebrates what Martin Buber calls the bond of the Absolute with
the particular, rather than with the general or the universal.

The Taoism of Lao-tzu (sixth century B.C.E.) is a mysticism of the
particular in which the concrete, precisely in its concreteness, reveals
vista upon vista to the eye of the person who meets it in openness. The
sound person, in consequence, is the one who does not try to capture
existence as a whole within the limited and limitedly useful categories
of analysis, whether scientific, psychoanalytic, or linguistic. Such a
person accepts life whole "without needing by measure or touch to
understand the measureless untouchable source of its images."

33

The metaphysician discriminates between the real world and mere "appearance" or "phenomena" and sets the goal of the true philosopher as ascending beyond the world of the senses to a face-to-face confrontation with absolute reality. Lao-tzu is content to allow the ultimate reality to speak to him in the only way in which it can speak to us humans—through its images. Although "the source" "appears dark emptiness," it actually:

> Brims with a quick force
> Farthest away
> And yet nearest at hand
> From oldest time unto this day,
> Charging its images with origin:
> What more need I know of the origin
> Than this?[2]

Men have called these living things "empty phenomena 'Meaningless images,' In a mirage / With no face to meet, / No back to follow." But that is because they insist on setting up a dualism between "mere appearance" and some entirely hidden, unmanifested Reality. "One who is anciently aware of existence / Is master of every moment." There is no split between the eternal and the present, the origin and the immediate in the openness in depth to what each moment tells of origin. Flowing with life, one "Feels no break since time beyond time / In the way life flows."[3]

In Zen Buddhism one finds the "essence" just as much in the movement of the world as in the nonmovement.

> Walking is Zen, sitting is Zen,
> Whether talking or remaining silent, whether moving or
> standing quiet, the essence itself is ever at ease.

34

In that sense, Zen is like Taoism: it does not cling to one opposite or the other.

> This very earth is the lotus land of purity,
> And this body is the body of the Buddha.
> The Buddha Nature, the particulars, and the no–
>   particulars are all one reality.
> There is nowhere in which the Way cannot be followed.[4]

To this type of mysticism of the particular also belongs the modern Jewish communal mysticism known as Hasidism, with its hallowing of the everyday.

"When I get to heaven," said Rabbi Zusya shortly before his death, "they will not ask me: 'Why were you not Moses?' but 'Why were you not Zusya?' " We are called to become what we in our created uniqueness can become—not just to fulfill our social duty or realize our talent or potentialities, but to become the unique person we are called to be. This is not an already existing unique-ness that we can fulfill through "self-expression" or "self-realiza-tion." We have to realize our uniqueness in response to the world. A part of this response, for Zusya, was the fact that Moses was there for him—not as a model to imitate, but as an image of the human that arose in dialogue, a "touchstone of reality" that entered into his own becoming.

When asked for one general way to the service of God, the Seer of Lublin replied:

> It is impossible to tell men what way they should take. For one way to serve God is through learning, another through prayer, another through fasting, and still another through eating. Everyone should carefully observe what way his heart draws him to, and then choose this way with all his strength.[5]

The way for the Hasid is not a matter of caste duty, or even of dharma or karma, but of one's personal uniqueness, one's "I" in the deepest sense of that term. To speak of the heart drawing us does not mean the facile impulse of the moment. Our "I" is not our image of ourselves but the deepest stirring within ourselves. That stirring, in its response, becomes our way.

Knowledge has to do with the general. Truth has to do with the unique. The unique does not mean the different, but the particular, that which is related to and for itself and as of value in itself. Rabbi Pinhas stressed that there is no person who is not incessantly being taught by his soul. "If this is so," asked one of his disciples, "why don't people obey their souls?" "The soul teaches incessantly," Rabbi Pinhas explained, "but it never repeats." The reason why the soul never repeats is that it does not teach in generalities but always only the message and demand of the unique situation in which the person finds himself.

When a woman came to Israel of Kosnitz to ask his help in bearing a son, he told her the story of a woman who had gone to the Baal Shem with a similar request. Asked what she was willing to do about it, the woman fetched her most precious possession, a fine cape. Finding the Baal Shem gone, she walked sixty verses from town to town to catch up with him and gave it to him, and then the whole way back. "A year later, I was born," said Rabbi Israel. "I too will bring you a good cape of mine so that I may get a son," the woman who had come to see him cried. "That won't work," the *maggid* (preacher) replied. "You heard the story. My mother had no story to go by."[6] The second woman wanted to take the unique response of the first and turn it into a general method that can be abstracted from the situation and objectified, an *omnicompetent technique* to be applied to all situations.

Schneur Zalman (d. 1813), the founder of the Habad, or Lubavitcher, Hasidism to which my mother's family belonged, once asked a disciple, "Moshe, what do we mean when we say 'God'?" The disciple was silent. After the *rav* had asked him a second and third time without response, he demanded the reason for his silence. "Because I do not know," replied the youth. "Do you think I know?" said the *rav*. "But I must say it, for it is so, and therefore I must say it: He is definitely there, and except for Him nothing is definitely there—and this is He." The *rav* could not define God, or describe his attributes, or even assert his existence in the abstract. But he could and did point in his dialogue with his disciple to meeting God in our actual existence in all its particularity. Once Shneur Zalman asked his son with what he prayed and was answered by a biblical verse belonging to the "spiritual" sphere. But when his son asked his father the same question, the *rav* answered, "I pray with the floor and the bench"[7]—the indispensable elements of the everyday world that sustained him in the midst of prayer as in his other activities. He did not have to leave the world to pray. On the contrary, it was only because he was firmly grounded in the world of particulars, the everyday world, that he could pray.

Also important for our purposes are a number of poets and thinkers who are almost equally well known as mystics. One such is the seventeenth-century English poet Thomas Traherne, a Western Christian mystic who discovers meaning in the meeting with the particular:

> Your enjoyment of the World is never right, till you so esteem it, that everything in it, is more your treasure than a King's exchequer full of Gold and Silver. . . . Some things are little on the outside, and rough and common, but I remember the time when the dust of the streets were as precious as Gold to my infant eyes, and now they are more precious to the eye of reason. . . .
>
> You never enjoy the world aright, till you see how a sand exhibiteth the wisdom and power of God. . . .

Your enjoyment of the world is never right, till every morning you awake in Heaven; see yourself in your Father's Palace; and look upon the skies, the earth, and the air as Celestial Joys. . . .

You never enjoy the world aright, till the Sea itself floweth in your veins, till you are clothed with the heavens, and crowned with the stars: and perceive yourself to be the sole heir of the whole world, and more than so, because men are in it who are every one sole heirs as well as you.[8]

Another modern mystic of the particular is the late eighteenth-century English poet William Blake (1757-1827), who spoke of seeing the universe in a grain of sand and exclaimed, "How do you know that every bird that wings its way through the air is not a whole world of delight closed to our senses five?" One example of Blake's strong sense of immanence of the divine is his poem "The Divine Image" from *The Songs of Innocence*. There we are told that mercy has a human heart, pity a human face, love the human form, and peace the human dress. From this the poet concludes that "all must love the human form in heathen, Turk or Jew" for where mercy, love, and pity dwell, there God is dwelling, too.[9]

Blake's praise of the "little lamb" is not inconsonant with his "Tyger, Tyger burning bright," as every schoolchild knows, even though the latter poem ends with a question that foreshadows our vision of the demonism of nature: "Did He who made the Lamb make thee?" Nothing in Blake's mysticism tempted him to say, like Alexander Pope earlier in the century, that whatever is is right because "we are but parts of one tremendous whole / Whose body nature is and God the soul." On the contrary, the chimney sweeper whom Blake celebrates in *The Songs of Innocence* ends his poem in *The Songs of Experience* with a condemnation of the divinely established social order that is built on his suffering: "And because I am happy, & dance & sing, / They think they have done me no injury; / And are gone to praise God & his Priest & King / Who make up a heaven of our misery."[10] Blake's greatest condemnation of the social evil found in the meeting with the particular is "London" where the chartered streets and mind-forged manacles are coupled with the chimney sweeper's cry, appalling the "blackning Church," and the sigh of hapless soldiers "runs in blood down Palace walls." But most of all the curse of youthful harlots "blasts the infant's tear and blights the marriage hearse!"[11]

To those who have become open to the closeness to the earth and to the sacred that is found in the traditions of Native Americans it should come as no surprise that the teachings of great Native Americans are permeated with the mysticism of the particular. The famous Suquamish chief Seattle, after whom the city is named, proclaims a bond between the red man and the soil of this country that the white man cannot know:

> Every part of this soil is sacred in the estimation of my people. Every hillside, every valley, every plain and grove, has been hallowed by some sad or happy event in days long vanished. Even the rocks, which seem to be dumb and dead as they swelter in the sun along the silent shore, thrill with memories of stirring events connected with the lives of my people, and the very dust upon which you now stand responds more lovingly to our footsteps than to yours, because it is rich with the blood of our ancestors and our bare feet are conscious of the sympathetic touch.[12]

Chief Luther Standing Bear tells of how the Lakota loved the earth and all things of the earth. Sitting or lying upon the ground, the old Indian "can see more clearly into the mysteries of life and come closer in kinship . . . with all creatures of the earth, sky and

39

water." "The old Lakota ... knew that man's heart away from nature becomes hard; he knew that lack of respect for growing, living things soon led to lack of respect for humans too."[13]

Ohiyesa, Santee Dakota physician and author, wrote in 1911 that prayer was the only inevitable duty—"the daily recognition of the Unseen and Eternal."

> His daily devotions were more necessary to him than daily food. He wakes at daybreak, puts on his moccasins and steps down to the water's edge. Here he throws handfuls of clear, cold water into his face, or plunges in bodily. After the bath, he stands erect before the advancing dawn. His mate may precede or follow him in his devotions, but never accompanies him. Each soul must meet the morning sun, the new sweet earth and the Great Silence alone!
>
> Whenever in the course of the daily hunt the red hunter comes upon a scene that is strikingly beautiful or sublime—a black thundercloud with the rainbow's glowing arch above the mountain, a white waterfall in the heart of a green gorge; a vast prairie tinged with the blood red of sunset—he pauses for an instant in the attitude of worship. He sees no need for setting apart one day in seven as a holy day, since to him all days are God's.[14]

The teaching of the nineteenth-century American poet Walt Whitman (1819-1892) is also that of a mysticism of the particular. In Whitman there is no asceticism and no putting off of the senses, as in St. John of the Cross' dark night of the senses and dark night of the soul, or in T. S. Eliot's *Four Quartets*. On the contrary, starting in *Leaves of Grass* with the celebration of himself, Whitman quickly expands it to include all the world in its particularity, for he identifies with everything, good and bad, that he has encountered. He bands together seen and unseen, what is known and what is mystery: "I and this mystery here we stand . . . and the unseen is proved by the seen, / Till that becomes unseen and receives proof in its turn."[15] This is quickly followed by his affirmation of belief in the flesh and its appetites and in seeing, hearing, and feeling as all miracles:

> Divine am I inside and out, and I make holy whatever I
>   touch or am touched from;
> The scent of these arm-pits is aroma finer than prayer,
> This head is more than churches or bibles or creeds.[16]

Then in a famous passage Whitman puts forth a "mysticism of the particular," closely akin to the spirit of Thomas Traherne, William Blake, Rabindranath Tagore, and Rainer Maria Rilke:

> I believe a leaf of grass is no less than the journeywork of
>   the stars,
> And the pismire is equally perfect, and a grain of sand,
>   and the egg of the wren,
> And the tree toad is a chef-d'oeuvre for the highest,
> And the running blackberry would adorn the parlors of
>   heaven. . . .[17]

In the end, Whitman wants to know nothing about God since he is quite satisfied with the God he knows in the everyday concrete. Like Gerard Manley Hopkins, he sees the Father in the features of men's faces:

> I who am curious about each am not curious about God,
> No array of terms can say how much I am at peace about
>   God and about death.
> I hear and behold God in every object, yet I understand

God not in the least,
Nor do I understand who there can be more wonderful
    than myself.
Why should I wish to see God better than this day?
I see something of God each hour of the twenty-four, and
    each moment then,
In the faces of men and women I see God, and in my own
    face in the glass;
I find letters from God dropped in the street, and every
    one of them is signed by God's name,
And I leave them where they are, for I know that others
    will punctually come forever and ever.[18]

Whitman's mysticism does not shy away from paradox: "Do I contradict myself? Very well then . . . I contradict myself; I am large . . . I contain multitudes."[19] In the end the persona of the poet becomes identical with that of the invisible God that permeates all the world of particulars:

I bequeath myself to the dirt to grow from the grass I love,
If you want me again look for me under your bootsoles.
You will hardly know who I am or what I mean,
But I shall be good health to you nevertheless,
And filter and fibre your blood.
Failing to fetch me at first keep encouraged,
Missing me one place search another,
I stop somewhere waiting for you.[20]

Although he cannot define his satisfaction or his life, he swears that every thing has an eternal soul and there is nothing but immortality and that all preparation, identity, and life and death are for it. "The soul is always beautiful, the universe is duly in order . . . every

42

thing in its place," and though "the diverse shall be no less diverse, they shall flow and unite now."[21]

Whitman's praise of wonder and the wonderful anticipates and is worthy of the poetic philosophy of Abraham Joshua Heschel and his "awareness of the ineffable." Whitman finds it wonderful that he is a six-foot, thirty-five-year-old man in 1855, that "my soul embraces you this hour" and we affect each other even though we may never meet, and that the moon and the earth balance themselves with the sun and stars.[22] Whitman's final affirmation in *Leaves of Grass* gives us an apt summation and conclusion:

> Great is life . . . and real and mystical . . . wherever and
>   whoever,
> Great is death. . . . Sure as life holds all parts together,
>   death holds all parts together;
> Sure as the stars return again after they merge in the
>   light, death is great as life.[23]

Whitman is justly famous for his egalitarianism, and this grows directly out of his mysticism of the particular—the absolute value of every "leaf of grass." This sets him in marked contrast to T. S. Eliot, who combines his mysticism with anti-egalitarian, hierarchical, nondemocratic social views.

The nineteenth-century English Catholic poet Francis Thompson is best known for his "Hound of Heaven." But it is his poem "In No Strange Land," or "The Kingdom of Heaven is Within You," that made such a strong impression on me that I used stanzas from it as an epigram for my book *Touchstones of Reality*. "O world invisible we view thee, / O world intangible we touch thee, / O world unknowable we know thee / Inapprehensible we clutch thee. // Does the fish soar to find the ocean / the eagle plunge to find the air / that we ask of the stars in motion / if they have rumor of Thee there? // Not where the wheeling systems darken, / and our benumbed conceiving soars / The drift of pinions would we hearken / Beats at our own clay-shuttered doors. // The angels keep their ancient places, / Turn but a stone and start a wing, / Tis ye, tis your estrangèd faces / That miss the many-splendoured thing! // But when so sad thou canst not sadder / Cry and on thy so sore loss / Shall shine the traffic of Jacob's ladder / Pitched between Heaven and Charing Cross. // Yea in the night, my soul my daughter, / Cry, clinging Heaven by the hems, / And lo Christ walking on the water / Not of Genessareth but Thames."

Another great nineteenth-century writer, Fyodor Dostoyevsky, gives a wonderful portrait of the best of Eastern Orthodox mysticism in Father Zossima, the *staretz*, or charismatic holy man, who occupies a central place in Dostoyevsky's last great novel *The Brothers Karamazov*. "Love all God's creation, the whole and every grain of sand in it. Love every leaf, every ray of light. Love the animals, love the plants, love everything," exhorts Father Zossima. We have here almost a nature mysticism. The secret of active love, says Zossima, is that it touches on the real mystery that binds everything together. "If you love everything, you will perceive the divine mystery in things . . . And you will come at last to love the whole world with an all-embracing love."

We have "a precious mystic sense of our living bond . . . with the higher heavenly world, and the roots of our thoughts and feelings are not here but in other worlds." Everything lives only through this mystic contact, and through this contact, too, each thing is in touch with each other thing. "My brother asked the birds to forgive him; that sounds senseless, but it is right; for all is like an ocean, all is flowing and blending; a touch in one place sets up movement at the other end of the earth." "Everything touches reciprocally," Zossima adds. This is a mysticism of active love. It does not posit an absolute unity of divine reality nor does it retreat within the soul to find reality. Rather, it finds the divine love in the reciprocal relationship of all being, in the "ocean, flowing and blending." This mysticism is not a denial of immediacy but its strongest affirmation, not a rejection of the material world but its transformation, not a turning away from the social world but its transfiguration. "If two of you are gathered together—then there is a whole world, a world of living love."[24]

Although Abraham Joshua Heschel is known as a Jewish philosopher of religion, he, too, is a modern mystic of the particular, as is shown by the very style of his writings. The rare quality of Heschel's own religious life—its dedicated intensity, poetic sensitivity, and serious concern—expressed itself again and again in passages in which artistic creativity, religious feeling, and mystical intuition are integrally united. Heschel's style is evocative of Thomas Traherne, Francis Thompson, and William Blake as well as Walt Whitman, to whom we have compared him. "What is intelligible to our mind is but a thin surface of the profoundly undisclosed, a ripple of inveterate silence that remains immune to curiosity and inquisitiveness like distant foliage in the dusk." "The universe is a score of eternal music and we are the cry, we are the voice." "There is so much light in our cage, in our world, it is as if it were suspended amidst the stars. Apathy turns to splendor unawares." "Inspiration passes; having been inspired remains . . . like an island across the restlessness of time, to which we move over the wake of undying wonder." Persons of faith "plant sacred thoughts in the uplands of time—the secret gardeners of the Lord in mankind's desolate hopes." In its startling imagery and paradoxical use of words, however, it resembles the styles of John Donne and T. S. Eliot. "Things are bereft of triteness." "They hear the stillness that crowds the world in spite of our noise." "We are rarely aware of the tangent of the beyond at the whirling wheel of experience." "Religion . . . comes to light . . . in moments of dis-

cerning the indestructibly sudden within the perishably constant."
"Faith is a blush in the presence of God." "Wonder is not a state
of aesthetic enjoyment," Heschel appropriately remarks. "Endless
wonder is endless tension, a situation in which we are shocked at
the inadequacy of our awe." "It is His otherness, ineffable and
immediate as the air we breathe and do not see, which enables us
to sense His distant nearness."

One way in which Heschel expressed his mysticism of the particular was his emphasis upon time as opposed to space, events as
opposed to process, divine presence as opposed to divine essence.
Heschel saw the world of space as "rolling through the infinite
expanse of time." Space constantly perishes, while time, though it
moves, is everlasting. "Time is the presence of God in the world of
space." We are called upon to sanctify our life in time rather than
the symbols of space; for the source of time is eternity. "To the
spiritual eye space is frozen time, and all things are petrified
events." We are the creatures of a Creator who creates the world
anew at every moment. Even our freedom is sustained in that
divine grace. We discover God's presence through the ineffable
that we encounter in all things, and in our response to the ineffable
we know ourselves as known by God. We find the meaning of our
lives not in ourselves, therefore, but in our relation to what transcends us. "To be is to stand for."[25]

From this brief glimpse of mystics of the particular we bear
with us several emphases: first, the uniqueness of each event or
experience; second, the discovery of meaning in the meeting with
the particular rather than through subsuming the particulars under
some overall plan, design, or worldview; and, third, the recognition
that the holy must be realized in our own place, "here where one
stands," "where one lets God in" by hallowing the everyday.

2

Poets of the Here and Now

Rilke's Ninth Duino Elegy

The late nineteenth and early twentieth century Prague poet Rainer Maria Rilke (1875-1926) is a very special sort of mystic of the particular. Despite some undoubted mystic experiences of which Rilke tells in letters and other writings, he does not easily fit our definition of mysticism. After the beautiful devotional poems *The Book of Hours* he has less and less to say of God, and even when he does, that God is neither expressible nor addressable but is, as Romano Guardini has pointed out, a quality of that highest love which Rilke sees as without a partner, or Thou, a love which alone leads us to that openness in which Rilke finds true human existence. Even the famous "angels" who are so central in the *Duino Elegies* are not messengers from God to man but strangely aloof beings who dwell in a dimension that we can never reach and who do not deign to notice us lest that notice destroy us utterly.

It might come as a surprise after all this to learn that the Welsh scholar B. J. Morse has conclusively proved an influence on Rilke of Buber's early Hasidic book *The Legend of the Baal-Shem,* an influence that manifests itself precisely in the Ninth Elegy,[1] with its magnificent expression of Rilke's peculiar, altogether unique, but nonetheless unmistakable mysticism of the particular. The passage that particularly influenced Rilke was the one on uniqueness from the *"Shiflut,"* or "Humility," section of Buber's "The Life of the Hasidim." Here Buber repeats again and again in the German original the word which Rilke takes over and himself hammers insistently in his elegy: "einmal." *Einmal* signifies one time only, unrepeatable, and unique, expounds Buber:

> That which exists is unique, and it happens but once. New and without a past, it emerges from the flood of returnings, takes place, and plunges back into it, unrepeatable. Each thing reappears at another time, but each transformed. . . . It is because things happen but once that the individual partakes in eternity. For the individual with his inextinguishable uniqueness is engraved in the heart of the all and lies forever in the lap of the timeless as he who is constituted thus and not otherwise.[2]

Humility is the love of a being who lives in a kingdom greater than the kingdom of the individual and speaks out of a knowing deeper than the knowing of the individual—the realm of "the between," which Buber equated even at this early date with God: "It exists in reality *between* the creatures, that is, it exists in God. Life covered and guaranteed by life."[3]

Rilke had that uniqueness and that "between" in his relationship to the world of things—to the panther and the rose and even "the unicorn," "the creature that does not exist." But he consciously turned aside from the between that might arise out of the meeting with the unique human Thou or with the divine Thou known in the between.[4] The Ninth Elegy speaks of the urgent command of the earth which wants to enter into the inwardness of the heart in order there to become "inner," to win the new dimension of reality. And man finds the meaning of his life in fulfilling this urgent command.

"*Hiersein ist herrlich*"—"To be here is splendid"—says the Seventh Elegy, and the Ninth shows why in an incomparably beautiful hymn of praise. This hymn begins with a lament which continues the thread of the previous elegy: "oh, why have to be human, and, shunning Destiny, long for Destiny?" Certainly not because of happiness, "that premature profit of imminent loss," or of curiosity, but because all of this fleeting Here and Now seems to require and concern us, the most fleeting of all. And here is where Rilke echoes Buber's song of uniqueness from *The Legend of the Baal-Shem*:

> Once and no more. And we, too,
> once. Never again. But this
> having been once, though only just once,
> on earth—can it ever be recalled? (vv.14-17)

Then the poet asks what can be brought over—not the art of seeing, or sufferings, or the hardness of life, or the experience of love; for all these things are purely untellable. We are perhaps here just for saying: House, Bridge, Fountain, Gate, Jug, Olive tree, Window in a way such as they themselves never hoped so intensely to be. The "sly purpose" of the earth even for lovers is to make everything leap with ecstasy within them. "*Here* is the time for the Tellable, *here* is its home." We cannot praise the untellable to the angel but only the world. We can show the angel some simple thing, remolded age after age till it lives in our hands and eyes as a part of ourselves. We can tell the angel *things*, and that will astonish him as they did us—how happy a thing can be, how innocent and ours. How a lamenting pain can disclose itself into shape, serve as a thing, or die into a thing. Although we are the "most fleeting of all," we can rescue the fleeting things and transform them entirely into ourselves.

The last stanza of the elegy is an invocation to the earth which, Rilke maintains, wants an invisible re-arising in us, dreams of being made invisible in us, urgently commands transformation. This stanza ends with a *cri de coeur*: A single spring is more than his blood can endure. "Supernumerous existence / wells up in my heart" (vv. 73-75, 79-80).[5]

Denise Levertov

In her poem "In California: Morning, Evening, Late January," Denise Levertov cries out, "Who can utter the poignance of all that is constantly threatened, invaded, expended. . . . Who can utter the praise of such generosity or the shame?"[6] But this motif was also present in her earlier poetry, as in "The Depths" where she speaks of "the abyss of everlasting light" which is revealed when the white fog burns off, the sacred salt that sparkles on our bodies after we have plunged into "the burning cold of ocean" and entered "an ocean of intense noon," and how all this recalls to us "the great depths about us."[7] And in "Come into Animal Presence" we feel the presence of the divine in the world of the particular more keenly still—the joy and guilelessness of the serpent, the rabbit, the llama, the armadillo: "Those who were sacred have remained so, . . . An old joy comes in holy presence."[8]

In "The Avowal" the particular of nature becomes the analogy for the simple faith that the poet would like to attain: She wants "to attain freefall and float / into Creator Spirit's deep embrace."[9]

An even greater simplicity of the particular is reached in "... That Passeth All Understanding":

> An awe so quiet
> I don't know when it began. //
> A gratitude
> had begun
> to sing in me. // ....
> When does night
> fold its arms over our hearts
> to cherish them?[10]

In "Of Being" the poet recognizes that her happiness is only provisional, for looming presences of great suffering and fear withdraw only into her peripheral vision. Nonetheless, she finds the shimmering of wind in the blue leaves, the flood of stillness widening the lake of sky, the need to dance and to kneel—all this mystery "ineluctable."[11] Levertov's poem "Passage" reminds us of Whitman's *Leaves of Grass* in the way it sees the spirit that walked upon the face of the waters as the one that walks the meadow of long grass so that "The grasses numberless, bowing and rising, silently / cry hosanna as the spirit / moves them." Her final line reminds one of Zen: "space and time are passing through like a swath of silk."[12]

Annie Dillard

The American poet and essayist Annie Dillard, though she throws in scientific facts that would do justice to a Loren Eiseley, says of herself that she is no scientist but "a wanderer with a background in theology and a penchant for quirky facts." I should say of her that she bends over the world with fervor so that the bestowing side of things leaps us to her, as Buber puts it in "With a Monist," and gives to her as prize the unique, the irreducible, the unrepeatable, the incomparable. "Beauty and grace are performed whether or not we will or sense them," she writes in *Pilgrim at Tinker Creek.* "The least we can do is try to be there." "Our life is a faint tracing on the surface of mystery, like the idle, curved tunnels of leaf miners on the face of a leaf." If we look and really describe what is going on in the whole landscape, "then we can at least wail the right question into the swaddling band of darkness, or, if it comes to that, choir the proper praise." Watching the running sheets of light raised on the creek's surface, "you yourself sail headlong and breathless under the gale force of the spirit."[13]

Following Heraclitus' suggestion that God neither declares nor hides but sets forth by signs, Dillard takes it as her task to scry the signs. One of the signs that she scries is time. "You cannot kill time without injuring eternity," she quotes from her reading. Dillard compares time to a child's toy slinky which walks uncannily down a lofty flight of stairs. Power and the spirit are like that, too. The spirit rolls along like the cereboros—the snake with its tail in its mouth. There are no hands to shake or edges to untie. The spirit "will not be trapped, slowed, grasped, fetched, peeled, or aimed."[14]

Another sign that Dillard scries is the Present. The door to the cedar tree that she sees may be *from* eternity, but it opens on to the real, present cedar, the particularity of time. " 'The scandal of particularity' is the only world that I, in particular, know," says Dillard. We're all up to our necks in this scandal. "I never saw a tree that was no tree in particular." Consciousness does not hinder our living in the present, for "it is only to a heightened awareness that the great door to the present opens at all." Only *self*-consciousness hinders our experience of the present. The present is more than a series of snapshots, and we are more than sensitized film. We have feelings, "eidetic memory for the imagery of our own pasts."[15] "This old rock planet gets the present for a present on its birthday; every day."

> The present is the wave that explodes over my head, flinging the air with particles at the height of its breathless unroll; it is the live water and light that bears from undisclosed sources the freshest news, renewed and renewing, world without end.[16]

Dillard knows that in order to scry the signs, she must herself be present and attentive, she must bring herself into the dialogue by bending over the world with fervor and evoking the bestowing side of things:

> At a certain point you say to the woods, to the sea, to the moun-tains, the world, Now I am ready. Now I will stop and be wholly attentive. You empty yourself and wait, listening. After a time you hear it: there is nothing there. There is nothing but those things only, those created objects, discrete, growing or holding, or swaying, being rained on or raining, held, flooding or ebbing, standing, or spread. You feel the world's word as a tension, a hum, a single chorused note everywhere the same. This it: this hum is the silence.[17]

In her essay on "Northing" Dillard says of herself that she wants to accomplish a kind of northing: "a single-minded trek toward that place where any shutter left open to the zenith at night will record the wheeling of all the sky's stars as a pattern of perfect, concentric circles. I seek a reduction, a shedding, a sloughing off." She accomplishes her "northing" extraordinarily well.[18]

Dillard, as we shall later see, also touches on the absurd. But she begins with an affirmation of the holy in the particular:

> Every day is a god, each day is a god, and holiness holds forth in time. I worship each god, I praise each day splintered down, splintered down and wrapped in time like a husk, a husk of many colors spreading, at dawn fast over the mountains split.[19]

Christ, the brown warm wind, hair, sky, beach, and shattered water have all fused into "one glare of holiness . . . bare and unspeakable." Now there is no one thing, motion, or time. "There is only this everything . . . and its bright and multiple noise."[20] At another point she witnesses that there are angels in those fields, in all fields and everywhere else, and swears that she would go to the lions for this conviction.[21]

Wendell Berry

Wendell Berry is a poet, novelist, essayist, and, like Annie Dillard, a nature lover, though without the "quirky facts." Berry is deep into the land and the farm that brings him close to the land and the dance of the living and dying who remain entwined with one another. In his early "Window Poems" he speaks of the rising of the river:

> It leaves a mystic plane
> in the air, a membrane

of history stretched between
the silt-lines on the banks,
a depth that for months
the man will go from his window
down into, knowing
he goes within the reach
of a dark power.

"The world is greater than its words," Berry tells us in the same poem. "To speak of it the mind must bend." Like Levertov, he is aware of "animal presence" and what we can learn from it:

Peace. Let men, who cannot be brothers
to themselves, be brothers
to mulleins and daisies
that have learned to live on the earth.
Let them understand the pride
of sycamores and thrushes
that receive the light gladly, and do not
think to illuminate themselves.
Let them know that the foxes and the owls
are joyous in their lives,
and their gayety is praise to the heavens,
and they do not raven with their minds.
In the night the devourer,
and in the morning all things
find the light a comfort.

At the end of the poem the window opens into the windowless, mystical whole:

He sits in the woods, watched
by more than he sees.
What is his is
past. He has come
to a roofless place
and a windowless.
There is a wild light
his mind loses
until the spring renews,
but it holds his mind
and will not let it rest.
The window is a fragment
of the world suspended
in the world, the known
adrift in mystery.
And now the green
rises. The window has an edge
that is celestial,
where the eyes are surpassed[22]

In his later poem "Woods" Berry contrasts his own silence, darkness, and heaviness with all that is around him:

I part the outthrusting branches
and come in beneath
the blessed and the blessing trees.
Though I am silent
There is singing around me.
Though I am dark
there is vision around me.
Though I am heavy
there is flight around me.[23]

56

This singing Berry hears in his own silence is echoed in "The Hidden Singer" where he goes beyond "the gods" to a spirit above and below them that needs nothing but its own wholeness, its health and ours. This spirit has made all things by dividing itself, yet it will be whole again. To its joy we come together—the seer and the seen; for in our joining it knows itself. It is "as a little bird / hidden in the leaves / who sings quietly / and waits / and sings."[24]

The spirit of this hidden little bird that waits and quietly sings is expanded into a full-fledged mystical vision of Creator and Creation toward the end of Berry's late poem "Elegy":

> "Our way is endless," my teacher said.
> "The Creator is divided in Creation
> for the joys of recognition. We knew
> that Spirit in each other once;
> it brings us here. By its divisions
> and returns, the world lives.
> Both mind and earth are made
> of what its light gives and uses up.
> So joy contains, survives its cost.
> The dead abide, as grief knows.
> We are what we have lost." //
> There is a song in the Creation;
> it has always been the gift
> of every gifted voice, though none
> ever sang it. As he spoke
> I heard that song. In its changes and returns
> his life was passing into life.
> That moment, earth and song and mind,
> the living and the dead, were one.[25]

In "The River Bridged and Forgot," a poem from a still later collection, Berry writes of his own work in a way that relates it to this mystical vision:

> Beside
> This dark passage of water
> I make my work, lifework
> of many lives that has
> no end, for it takes circles
> of years, of birth and death
> for pattern, eternal form
> visible in mystery.
> It takes for pattern the heavenly
> and earthly song of which
> it is a part, which holds it
> from despair: the joined voices
> of all things, all muteness
> vocal in their harmony.
> For that, though none can hear
> or sing it all, though I
> must by nature fail,
> my work has turned away
> the priced infinity
> of mechanical desire.[26]

A fitting conclusion to these selections is what Berry says about the dance and love in the middle stanza of his 1982 poem "Passing the Strait":

> The dance passes beyond us,
> our loves loving their loves,
> and returns, having passed through

the breaths and sleeps of the world,
the woven circuits of desire,
which leaving here arrive here.
Love moves in a bright sphere.[27]

All these poems are one in spirit with the mystical vision with which Berry concludes his 1988 novel, *Remembering*. A very down-to-earth novel if a deeply moving one, *Remembering* has a remarkable mystical ending. The hero, Andy, has left his Kentucky farm home for San Francisco to run away not only from his family and his life but also from himself, which he can no longer accept now that he has lost his right hand through an accident while operating farm machinery. The novel is a series of rememberings, not only of his own personal past life but of those of others whom he has known or known of through the memories that have been handed down. So there is already a collective remembered reality that has much to do with his finally accepting and being healed and paves the way for the collective mysticism of the ending.

At the end of the novel, when he sees himself as "a nothing possessed of a terrible self-knowledge," he is awakened from his hopeless dark sleep by what feels like the pressure of a hand. He is where he was, in the valley, but the place is transformed. "The birds sing a joy that is theirs and his, and neither theirs nor his." He follows a dark man along a narrow ancient track in the almost dark to a hillside where he hears, above and beyond the birds' song, a distant singing which fills the sky and touches the ground, and the birds answer it. He hears the light of the sun and of all things:

The light's music resounds and shines in the air and over the countryside, drawing everything into the infinite, sensed but mysterious pattern of its harmony. From every tree and leaf, grass blade, stone, bird, and beast, it is answered and again answers in return. The creatures sing back their names. But more than their names. They sing their being. The world sings. The sky sings back. It is one song, the song of the many members of one love, the whole song sung and to be sung, resounding, in each of its moments. And it is light.[28]

Looking where the dark man points, he sees his home—Port William and the countryside—"as he never saw or dreamed them, the signs everywhere upon them of the care of a longer love than any who have lived there have ever imagined." Over the town and fields the one great song sings and is answered everywhere: "every leaf and flower and grass blade sings." This presence extends to the people, too, who are of such beauty that he weeps to see them.

> He sees that these are the membership of one another and of the place and of the song or light in which they live and move.
> He sees that they are the dead, and they are alive. He sees that he lives in eternity as he lives in time, and nothing is lost. . . . The young are no longer young, nor the old old. They appear as children corrected and clarified; they have the luminous vividness of new grass after fire. And yet they are mature as ripe fruit. And yet they are flowers. All of them are flowers.[29]

Andy would like to go to them, but he knows he must go back to his life "with his help, such as it is, and offer it." He knows that all this has taken place through a change of sight. As he prepares to leave them, their names are singing in his mind, and "he lifts toward them the restored right hand of his joy."

Both the mystics of the particular and the poets of the here and

60

now care for the unique, for that which is ultimately unrationalizable yet can be directly known in the "between"—not through theological creeds or faith but through contact, immediacy, relationship.

Part Two

Evil and the Absurd:
The Threat of
Meaninglessness

The Shattering of Security

Melville's *Moby Dick*

What we are confronted with in modern literature is not merely the loss of faith in the face of intellectual doubt. Deeper than this lies the shattering of the security which we are given by social custom, worldviews, or the sense of order that our religion or personal philosophy has bequeathed us. Jude does not go through an intellectual process of doubt in Thomas Hardy's *Jude the Obscure*. He dies alone and abandoned with Job's curse of the day of his birth on his lips because of the bitter disappointments and betrayals he has experienced in his life. Even where the issue of faith is posed intellectually, as in Melville and Dostoyevsky, what undergirds it is the shattering of security, the loss of existential trust.

In *Moby Dick* it is the changing relationship of truth and reality which takes us out to sea and in the end turns us back toward home. It is this relation which is the very dynamism of the book, correlative with the basic symbolism of sea and land. The land is the harbor, the sea is the open, perilous part of the world. The sea is that toward which we go in search of truth till we are no longer able to face the truth, or until truth is sundered from reality, and our only choice is to be drowned in reality or to retreat to land without our full share of the truth. This is the paradox through which Melville expresses the "death of God."

What Copernicus and Pascal stated of space, Ishmael states of time: that man is not its center, that human life shrinks into itself in terror before the vision, preeminently accorded to modern man, of time stretching indefinitely into the past and the future. The special terror in the modern vision of evil is that it is completely impersonal. *"Le silence éternel de ces espaces infinis m'effraie"* (the eternal silence of these infinite spaces frightens me), says Pascal in *Les Pensées*. Behind Ishmael's imageless god is not the God of Job who can speak to man out of the whirlwind but the "dead God" who cannot speak at all—the god who is no god.

The "awful lonesomeness" of the open, shoreless ocean "is intolerable," says Ishmael. "The intense concentration of self in the middle of such a heartless immensity, my God! who can tell it?" The "heartless immensity" of the ocean, no less than "the heartless voids and immensities of the Universe" ("The Whiteness of the Whale"), forces us to realize our own limitedness, our own mortality. When one loses one's limits, when one can no longer retain one's inwardness and at the same time relate to the world outside, one has lost that condition that makes human existence possible. The indifference of the universe means the annihilation of all human value, for it is a denial of human personality in its unrepeatable uniqueness. At its deepest level *Moby Dick* is a recognition of the tragic limitations that are encountered by modern man since the Renaissance. These are the limits of existence, the limits of creation with which God "taunts" Job.

Chinua Achebe's *Things Fall Apart*

The shattering of security is also dramatically embodied in Chinua Achebe's *Things Fall Apart*. The title of this novel is taken from the first stanza of W. B. Yeats's famous poem "The Second Coming":

> Turning and turning in the widening gyre
> The falcon cannot hear the falconer;
> Things fall apart; the centre cannot hold;
> Mere anarchy is loosed upon the world,
> The blood-dimmed tide is loosed, and everywhere
> The ceremony of innocence is drowned;
> The best lack all conviction, while the worst
> Are full of passionate intensity.[1]

This "classic of modern African writing" is described on the cover of this edition as "the story of a 'strong' man whose life is dominated by fear and anger, a powerful and moving narrative that critics have compared with classic Greek tragedy." The comparison with Greek tragedy is aptly made since Okonkwo, its hero, is truly a hero in the classic sense of the term and one who possesses a flaw—fear and anger—which brings about a downfall greater than he deserved. Another way of putting it is that he is a self-made man who goes from winning a wrestling championship that makes him famous in all the villages of the Ibo when he is young to becoming an established leader of his tribe; yet he cannot withstand the changes that come when the whites arrive with their Christian missionaries and their centralized power. As someone said of a well-known college president who died of a heart attack during a student sit-down strike in the turbulent sixties in the United States, "He would not bend, so he broke."

But on deeper reflection, we cannot call this a Greek tragedy since the true Greek tragedy presupposed an order, *moira*, with which the tragic hero became reconciled even at the price of suffering and death. Okonkwo is perhaps closer to Melville's Captain Ahab, who defies an order that does not include him, except that Melville does it on the basis of his own Promethean stance, whereas Okonkwo, like Sophocles' Antigone, defies the new order on the basis both of the tribal order in which he prospered *and* of the place which he had forged for himself in that order.

In no case is that larger order that Yeats envisioned in his mystical-occult work *The Vision* in question here. To Yeats the approaching year 2000 (a great deal closer to us than it was to Yeats when he wrote the poem seventy years ago in the aftermath of the First World War) meant the nadir in the historical cycle that found its zenith in the birth of Christ—both events subsumed under the phases of the moon and the pull of opposites in human life and in history. "The Second Coming's" just fame has nothing to do with all this but only with that "mere anarchy" which is loosed upon the world when the old order dies and no new one has yet been born or is even in prospect. Okonkwo is surely one of "the worst" who are "full of passionate intensity," but he is also, paradoxically, one of the best. He does not "lack all conviction," as Yeats has it, but his conviction is questionable—not because of the tribal order on which he grounds it but because of the super-macho stance which he has adopted to counteract the weakness and ineptness in his father which shamed him.

Okonkwo is the victim of this very stance. Like all macho men, he also insists that his sons be macho. But he alienates his own first son, Nwoye, in a way that is indeed tragic in Buber's sense of two who cannot meet because each is as he is. Okonkwo, of course, cannot tolerate difference or uniqueness in his son and complains from the start that Nwoye is too sensitive and too like a girl, whereas his eldest daughter should have been a boy. This sensitivity leads Nwoye to sadness and compassion when he sees the twins who have been murdered in the bush according to Ibo tribal custom.

More salient still for him is the fate of Ikemefuna, a boy from another tribe who has been given as a hostage in exchange for an injury that someone in that tribe did to Okonkwo's tribe. The boy is sent to live with Okonkwo until it is decided what to do with him, and this stretches on for years, during which time he becomes a son to Okonkwo and an older brother to Nwoye. After some time, the elders of the tribe consult the oracle and decide that Ikemefuna must die. Ikemefuna is told that he is going home and sets out with the elders on the voyage. One elder, who knows what is happening, goes to Okonkwo and warns him not to go with them, saying "That boy has called you father." But Okonkwo thinks it necessary to display his manliness even here, and not only accompanies them but, when Ikemefuna turns to him for help, kills him himself with his own machete.

The result is that when the Christian missionaries come, Nwoye goes to join them, to the great horror of his father who feels that this is the action both of a traitor and a girl. And it is the intrusion of this new religion, with the not too well disguised violence and power that enforces its "Christian love," that leads by a series of steps to Okonkwo's own downfall. The elders of the tribe burn down the church; they are held for a period by the whites and by blacks of other tribes who treat them brutally.

Among these elders is Okonkwo, who has only recently returned from seven years' exile in another tribe because of having accidentally killed a fellow tribesman. Okonkwo wants them all to organize to fight the whites and their black henchmen, but he finds no one willing to stand with him. At the very moment when Okonkwo is trying unsuccessfully to stir the other elders up to "bale this water now that it is only ankle-deep," five court messengers (themselves black) come upon them from the white man's court. Okonkwo bars the way of the head messenger who demands to be let past. When Okonkwo asks him what he wants here, the head messenger replies, "The white man whose power you know too well has ordered this meeting to stop." At this Okonkwo draws his machete in a flash and severs the man's head from his body.

The rest does indeed proceed with the inevitableness of a Greek tragedy. When the district commissioner arrives at Okonkwo's compound at the head of an armed band of soldiers and court messengers, the small crowd of men who are sitting wearily in the *obi* take him to the tree where Okonkwo has hanged himself and ask their help in cutting him down and burying him, since tribal law forbids their burying someone who has killed himself. Okonkwo's friend Obierika, after gazing at Okonkwo's hanging body, turns to the district commissioner and says ferociously: "That man was one of the greatest men in Umofia. You drove him to kill himself; and now he will be buried like a dog," summing up the tragedy as well as anyone could.

The second missionary who comes there has no interest in understanding, much less engaging in dialogue with, the native religion; but the first, Mr. Brown, is a man of different cloth. Whenever he comes to the village, he spends hours talking to Akunna, one of the great men in that village who had given one of his sons to be taught the white man's knowledge in Mr. Brown's school. They talk through an interpreter, and what they talk about is religion. "Neither of them succeeded in converting the other but they learned more about their different beliefs," says the author. We can say more: They actually approach one another in Akunna's explanation that the native idols are not just pieces of wood and that the lesser gods stand in for but do not replace awareness of the one great god.

"In my religion [said Mr. Brown] Chukwu is a loving Father and need not be feared by those who do His will."

"But we must fear Him when we are not doing His will," said Akunna. "And who is to tell His will? It is too great to be known."[2]

What Akunna says is remarkably close to good Christian doctrine. In any case, here in the midst of the larger and tragic mismeeting which gives form to this novel, there is one real meeting and one genuine dialogue between two religious orders that one might have thought (and that Mr. Brown himself obviously originally supposed) could not meet.

But Akunna's final statement about the will of God brings to mind a statement by Franz Kafka:

Only those fear to be put to the proof who have a bad conscience. They are the ones who do not fulfill the tasks of the present. Yet who knows precisely what his task is? No one. So that every one of us has a bad conscience.[3]

4

Faith, Anguish, and Doubt

Dostoyevsky's Ivan Karamazov

In many modern writers the shattering of security expresses itself in the anguished tension between faith and doubt. This struggle has never been bodied forth more dramatically in literature than in the figure of Ivan in Dostoyevsky's great novel *The Brothers Karamazov*. Ivan is a man of ideas, but the ideas are all dialectical ones, swinging between pole and pole. Ivan's tales of sadistic, sensual brutality (such as that of the general who had his dogs tear a serf boy to pieces before the eyes of his mother because the boy had thrown a stone that injured the paw of a favorite greyhound) lead him to conclude that underlying man is irrational violence.

> In every man, of course, a demon lies hidden—the demon of rage, the demon of lustful heat at the screams of the tortured victim, the demon of lawlessness let off the chain.[1]

But the injured image of the human also means an injured image of the divine. "I think if the devil doesn't exist, but man has created him, he has created him in his own image and likeness," Ivan says to his brother Alyosha and adds laughingly, "Yours must be a fine God if man created Him in His image and likeness." The God who created man must be a devil, Ivan implies, stating in his own way Melville's assertion that the loss of trust in man means a loss of trust in man's creator.

If even his pious and gentle brother Alyosha agrees that the general should be shot "for the satisfaction of our moral feelings," then it proves, says Ivan, that "the world stands on absurdities, and perhaps nothing would have come to pass in it without them." In his emphasis on the absurd and the irreducible particular, Ivan clearly anticipates the modern existentialist. "If I try to understand anything, I shall be false to the fact," declares Ivan, "and I have determined to stick to the fact." Ivan's "fact" is the unique existing person whose life and happiness he refuses to subsume under any general plan, no matter how beneficently conceived. Why should the little child who has been shut in a privy all night and whose mother has rubbed its face with feces and put them in its mouth "beat her little aching heart with her tiny fist in the dark and the cold, and weep her meek unresentful tears to dear, kind God to protect her?" Like the Danish existentialist theologian Søren Kierkegaard, Ivan refuses to see the Single One *sub specie aeternitatis*. Seen from the standpoint of the universal, the individual person has meaning only in terms of that universal. Seen from his own standpoint, however, a knowledge of good and evil which reveals itself to be diabolical is not worth the cost.

I must have justice, or I will destroy myself. And not justice in some remote infinite time and space, but here on earth, and that I could see myself. . . . Surely I haven't suffered, simply that I,

74

my crimes and my suffering, may manure the soil of the future harmony for somebody else.[2]

Ivan's rebellion is not the rejection of the transcendent for the sake of the immanent, like that of Nietzsche and Sartre. It is the much more terrible rebellion of Job, who curses the day of his birth and questions the very meaning of his existence. Like Captain Ahab, Ivan has nothing of Job's answer, even though he starts with Job's question. Yet in his demand that God be real for this world, the atheist Ivan is far closer to Job than those who have forgotten the present world for the promise of a future harmony, religious or secular, or have "adjusted" themselves to the world and ceased to care about its evil and suffering. Ivan says that he accepts God, but he cannot accept his world and the eternal harmony in which, in some indefinite future, the sufferings of all the generations of mankind will somehow be reconciled and redeemed. He knows that no meaning attained in the future can make up for the lack of meaning in the present.

Like Job, Ivan demands that he himself see: "I want to see with my own eyes the hind lie down with the lion and the victim rise up and embrace his murderer." If he cannot see it, if his Euclidean, three-dimensional mind cannot understand such mysteries, then he rejects this harmony and hastens to return to God the "entrance ticket" for which he has asked too high a price. "From love of humanity I don't want it. . . . I would rather remain with my unavenged suffering and unsatisfied indignation, *even if I were wrong.*"

Emily Dickinson

There is probably no modern poet whose poetry is more liberally sprinkled with explicit religious motifs than Emily Dickinson— death, Christ, resurrection, immortality, eternity, God, the Day of Judgment, angels, souls, the grave, the church. All befitting the daughter of a New England pastor and all are enough to gladden the heart of any nineteenth-century preacher or theologian. Yet she deserves a place in this chapter through her subtle and exquisite combination of faith and doubt, two separate vines that are entwined and entangled, but that are both rooted in Dickinson's own basic attitudes. "Doubt" here does not mean agnosticism, questioning the existence of God. Quoting Eugenia Friedman, "Dickinson's 'love' is imperfect—she is disloyal, she questions His ways, she is accusatory, and worst of all, ironic. But she does relate."

Sometimes Dickinson is whimsical, as when she states that "faith is a fine invention when gentlemen can *see* / but microscopes are prudent in an emergency," or when she speaks of transport, ecstasy, and rapture as sideshows which the universe would go to see, along with "Holy Ghosts in Cages!" At other times she hints darkly of "a certain slant of light" that "oppresses like cathedral tunes" and gives us "Heavenly Hurt," not with outer scars but "internal difference, / Where Meanings are—." It is sealed by despair, and when it goes it is like "the Distance / On the Look of Death—."

When we come on explicit doubt in Dickinson, it is the doubt not of the rationalist and skeptic but of one who has known enough suffering in life to question whether there can, indeed, be a heavenly recompense to balance it:

76

I reason, Earth is short—
And Anguish—absolute—
And many hurt,
But, what of that? //
I reason, we could die—
The best Vitality
Cannot excel Decay,
But, what of that? //
I reason, that in Heaven—
Somehow, it will be even—
Some new Equation, given—
But, what of that?[4]

Sometimes faith and doubt seem to be perfectly balanced on the seesaw of Dickinson's poems, as when she speaks of being too rescued in the face of Jesus' prayer on the cross of being forsaken, earth too much, heaven not enough, "so Savior—Crucify," all to end with, " 'Faith' bleats—to understand!" as if faith of this sort were nothing more than a bleating lamb or goat that cannot begin to grasp the reality of what it utters. Or as when she speaks of testing our horizon with a retrospection of fixed delight and an anticipation of doubt, or of death as a dialogue between spirit and dust.[5]

At other times, though, the doubt seems to come through unalloyed, precisely in the game that God plays with us:

I know that He exists.
Somewhere—in Silence—
He has hid his rare life
From our gross eyes. // . . .
[But] should the glee—glaze—
In Death's—stiff—stare— //
Would not the fun
Look too expensive!
Would not the jest—
Have crawled too far![6]

One motif that occurs often in Dickinson's poetry is that of great pain, which she likens to that which "He . . . bore . . . Yesterday, or Centuries before." At other times the comparison gives way to an abyss, as when she pictures God's caring as much about her prayer as he might if a bird stamped its foot on the air and cried, "Give Me"! At other times she exposes the fragility of faith, which unlike real estate cannot be replenished and, though inherited with life, can be annihilated at one blow so that being becomes beggary.[7]

Since so much of Dickinson's poetry is surprising, it should not surprise us that some of Dickinson's poems about faith and doubt seem to start with faith yet end with a curious twist that leaves us in doubt. In one poem she pictures herself with modest needs and a single prayer asking for a heaven just large enough for herself. She receives a remarkable approving, even twinkling response, from Jehovah, the Cherubim, the Great Saints, and even Judgment, all extolling her honesty and seeming to promise that whatever she asks will be given to her. Yet she ends on a decidedly skeptical note:

> But I, grown shrewder—scan the Skies
> With a suspicious Air—
> As Children—swindled for the first
> All Swindlers—be—infer—[8]

In what is probably the most famous of her poems, a faith seems to be embodied: As she never saw a moor or the sea, yet knows what heathers and billows look like, so she has never spoken with God nor visited heaven yet is certain "of the spot."[9]

After all this it would not be amiss to close with two poems about truth and skepticism that show how essentially opaque Dickinson's point of view is—a case, if ever, where the religious attitude is inseparable from the poetry itself. In one she speaks of the sweet skepticism of the heart that knows and does not know, invites and retards the Truth "Lest Certainty be sere."[10] In the other, she offers an approach to truth remarkably similar to that of Ishmael in *Moby Dick* with his repeated concern that we look not too close lest we go blind or be "eternally stove in":

> Tell all the Truth but tell it slant—
> Success in Circuit lies
> Too bright for our infirm Delight
> The Truth's superb surprise //
> As Lightning to the Children eased
> With explanation kind
> The Truth must dazzle gradually
> Or every man be blind—[11]

Gerard Manley Hopkins

To move from Emily Dickinson to Gerard Manley Hopkins is not to move to greater faith and still less to doubt, but to a purer and more passionate expression of faith mixed with a depth of anguish that Dickinson does not attain. In addition there is in Hopkins' poems a poignant awareness of both human suffering and human evil. Hopkins' most famous poems seem to be pure and unalloyed praise, as in "Spring" with its exclamation, "What is all this juice and all this joy?" and its counsel to "innocent mind and Mayday in girl and boy" to enjoy this Eden garden that spring offers before it "cloy, cloud, and sour with sinning." Or "Pied Beauty" which begins with "Glory be to God for dappled things" and ends with "He fathers-forth whose beauty is past change: Praise him."[12]

There are more complex statements of praise, too, as in "God's Grandeur" which contrasts the world "charged with the grandeur of God" with the generations who have seared, bleared, and smeared it with their treading, only to end with the affirmation that "there lives the dearest freshness deep down things . . . Because the Holy Ghost over the bent / World broods with warm breast and with ah! bright wings." Another such complex statement of praise is "The Windhover," the rapture over the hovering and the rapid plummeting of a falcon which, even if it had not been dedicated "To Christ our Lord," we should recognize as a celebration of that meaning and joy which is found only after great suffering and pain. The fire that breaks from the falcon when it plummets is a billion times lovelier and more dangerous, just as the sheer plodding of the horses makes the "plough down sillion shine" and the falling of the blue-bleak embers in the fire makes them gall and gash themselves "gold-vermillion."[13]

A far more sustained and balanced contrast is given us by

"The Leaden Echo" with its lament for the passing of the "girl-graces" of youth, and "The Golden Echo" with its breathtaking evocation of a lasting reality before which we must resign our winning ways and give our beauty "back to God, beauty's self and beauty's giver." Here Hopkins repeats Jesus' statement of faith from the Gospels, "See; not a hair is, not an eyelash, not the least lash lost; every hair is, hair of the head, numbered" and goes beyond Jesus with a preservation of the human event that moves from the biblical *emunah*, or unconditional trust, which Jesus proclaimed to an almost Whiteheadian faith in a God who conserves the lasting reality of process.

> Nay, what we had lighthanded left in surly the mere mould
> > Will have waked and have waxed and have walked with the
> wind what while we slept.

We who are "so haggard at the heart, so care-coiled, care-killed, so fagged, so fashed, so cogged, so cumbered," what we freely forfeit is kept "Yonder" with far fonder a care than we could have had.[14]

On the other hand, there are a number of Hopkins's poems that, while they do not express doubt in the sense of disbelief, have almost no balance on the side of positive affirmation of faith, so deep is their anguish and despair. One of the most powerful of these is "Spelt from Sibyl's Leaves" which tells us of an earth whose being has come unbound and whose dapple (note the contrast with "Pied Beauty") is at an end and of a self so steeped in self that in the middle of the poem comes, "Heart, you round me right with: Our évening is over us; our night whélms, whélms, and will end us," and at the end, we are told of "a rack where, self-wrung, selfstrung, sheathe- and shelterless, thoughts against thoughts in groans grind."[15]

While not so unremittingly bleak as this oracle, the three

poems which we shall look at now are overwhelming in their naked personal anguish, which has nothing to do with intellectual doubt but much to do with that sense of forsakenness which Dickinson enunciated. "Carrion Comfort" begins with a resolution not to feast on despair even though he can cry no more and "not choose not to be." Why must thou "rude on me" and "lay a lionlimb against me," cries the poet? During that year of now done darkness he kissed the rod and "I wretch lay wrestling with (my God!) my God." In a second poem, "I wake to feel the fell of dark, not day." The poet thinks of the black hours he has spent that night as years, even a lifetime.

> I am gall, I am heartburn. God's most deep decree
> Bitter would have me taste; my taste was me. . . .
> Selfyeast of spirit a dull dough sours. I see
> The lost are like this, and their scourge to be
> As I am mine, their sweating selves; but worse."[16]

The third poem is a real contending with God ("Thou art indeed just, Lord, if I contend with Thee") worthy of Job, complaining about the prospering of sinners' ways and the disappointment of all he undertakes. "Wert thou my enemy, O thou my friend, / How wouldst thou worse, I wonder, than thou dost / Defeat, thwart me?" Birds build, but all the poet does is strain, "time's eunuch," who does "not breed one work that wakes." The poem ends with a deeply moving prayer that is not so much an affirmation of faith as a plea for grace: "Mine, O thou lord of life, send my roots rain."[17]

Denise Levertov

With Levertov, instead of anguish and total commitment to God, as in Hopkins, we find doubt and a deep caring about the earth and her fellow human beings. Only one segment of her poetry seems to be religious, whereas the whole of Dickinson and Hopkins is. Given this, a surprising amount of Denise Levertov's poetry is not only explicitly religious but explicitly Christian. Her father was an Eastern European Jew who wrote a book on Hasidism in the earlier years of this century but then converted and became an Anglican clergyman after he moved to England, where Levertov grew up. Levertov has set her quintessential expression of faith and doubt in the context of the figure who has come down through the ages as "doubting Thomas," Jesus' disciple who said that he would not believe in the resurrection until he had put his hand in the wounds. "I see, Lord, and I believe," he is said to have exclaimed, to which the risen Christ is said to have responded, "You have seen and you have believed. But blessed are those who have not seen and yet believe."

Levertov celebrates this event in a "Mass for the Day of St. Thomas Didymus." In the Kyrie she prays that the deep, remote unknown have mercy on us who live in terror both of what we know and what we do not know, our own and the world's death, which we both imagine and cannot imagine, of the freefalling into which our dread sinks or the violent closure of all. Our hope, she enigmatically states, lies in the unknowing. In the Gloria she praises the early falling snow and the shadow from her neighbor's chimney, the invisible sun, and the unknown gods who stay our murderous hands and give us, in the shadow of death, our daily life so that we can dream of goodwill and peace on earth. In the Credo she affirms her belief that each "minim mote" of the earth's dust is the holy glory of God's candle and, like the ancient Church father, she prays God to help her in her unbelief. "I believe and interrupt my belief with doubt. I doubt and interrupt my doubt with belief."

In the Sanctus Levertov prays that all that Imagination has wrought in the throes of epiphany to give to the Vast Loneliness a locus and a hearth should send forth its song toward the harboring silence, uttering "the multiform name of the Other, the known Unknown, unknowable." In Benedictus she asks, "What of the emptiness, the destructive vortex that whirls no word with it?" and adds, "But can the name utter itself in the downspin of time? Can it enter the void?" Her final affirmation is a mixture of faith and doubt: "The word chose to become flesh. In the blur of flesh we bow, baffled." In Agnus Dei Levertov plays on the metaphor of the lamb of God that takes away the Sins of the World to ask how God could become an innocence smelling of ignorance, how all-encompassing God could be defenseless and omnipotent God reduced to a wisp of damp wool. Does all this imply that we, frightened, bored, wanting only to sleep, we with our shamefaced private hope of being given a bliss we deserve only because we imagine it, *we* must protect and hold to our icy hearts a shivering God? Levertov's conclusion is not, like Archibald Macleish's in *J.B.*, that the light has gone out in the sky and in the church but can still be kindled and brought to life in the human heart. Rather she takes seriously the transcendence *and* the helplessness of the suffering God and our human task in relation to this exiled divinity:

> Come rag of pungent
> quiverings,
>   dim star.
>   Let's try
> if something human still
>   can shield you,

spark
of remote light.[19]

In "St. Thomas Didymus," which appears to be a somewhat
later poem, Levertov sees herself as twin to the man that she hears
cry out weeping and speaking those same words, "Lord, I believe,
help thou mine unbelief." She sees him as someone whose whole
being has knotted itself into one tightdrawn question: Why is this
man tormented, torn, twisted? "Why is he cruelly punished who
has done nothing except be born?" His question becomes her
question, throbbing like a stealthy cancer, and staying with her in
convulsed writhings even after Golgotha, the empty tomb, and the
hope that came with the touch of blood that told her the truth. Even
the sight of the dark crust round the nailholes could not unloose
that knot that came from the battle she fought with life. But then
when the poet's hand enters the unhealed wound and feels rib-
bone and pulsing heart, she does not feel scalding pain or shame
for her obstinate need but transforming light streaming over her
and filling the room, unravelling the knot within her so that her
question was "not answered but given its part in a vast unfolding
design lit by a risen sun."[19]

Except for the Dantesque and, in my view, questionable "part
in a vast unfolding design," this is a marvelous example of a faith
which makes the religious event of the past present in such a way
that it can take the deep existential doubt into itself and become
an affirmation of all ages and of the present. If one reads the liturgy
that Levertov wrote for archbishop Cesar Romero and the four
nuns assassinated in El Salvador, one glimpses out of what depths
of anguish and doubt this affirmation has risen.

In "Flickering Mind" Levertov expresses her tension between faith
and doubt directly, personally, and without the mediation of doubting
Thomas. It is not you but I who am absent, she says to the Lord:

At first
belief was a joy I kept in secret,
stealing alone
into sacred places:
a quick glance, and away—and back,
circling.
I have long since uttered your name
but now
I elude your presence.
I stop
to think about you, and my mind
at once
like a minnow darts away

Her self will not hold still for a second but wanders anywhere and everywhere that it can turn. This is a new kind of "Lord I believe, help Thou my unbelief!":

you the unchanging presence, in whom all
moves and changes.
How can I focus my flickering, perceive
at the fountain's heart
the sapphire I know is there?[20]

5

The Demonism of Nature

Especially in modern times but also throughout human existence, it is the encounter with evil that has given rise more than anything to the tension and struggle between faith and doubt. But if this encounter has tested the religious in its depth, it has also evoked it. No metaphysics, philosophy of religion, or theodicy can compare with literature in its power of setting evil before us and of bodying forth the answering response that has arisen time and again from the depths of human existence. It is not surprising, therefore, that the shattering of security that we have seen so graphically portrayed in *Moby Dick* should be so closely entwined at every point with the encounter with evil.

In "The Whiteness of the Whale" (LXII) the whiteness of Moby Dick is subsumed under the all-encompassing paradox of whiteness in general. Whiteness is at once the very color of the divinity and the color of everything that is most terrifying. At first "the visible world seems formed in love," but then the revelation comes that "the invisible spheres were formed in fright"—and it is all the more horrible because it is a later revelation. Whiteness is "the most meaning symbol of spiritual things, nay, the very veil of the Christian's Deity," and yet it is "the intensifying agent in things the most appalling to mankind." The evil, which at first seems a small part of our existence, turns out to be its great underlying reality. Either we must deny it or we must ascribe it to God, neither of which we can do. Therefore the universe breaks apart; it is no longer a *uni*verse at all, but simply man and the "inscrutable malice" opposite him. Whiteness is "the colorless, all-color of atheism." Like the traveler to Lapland who refuses to use colored glasses, "so the wretched infidel gazes himself blind at the monumental white shroud that wraps all the prospect around him." If one looks at reality without rose-colored glasses, if one looks the truth in the face, one must go blind. One cannot see the truth and live; or rather there is no longer any truth, for reality is too much for us.

Our ordinary assumption is that truth and reality are synonymous. As we have seen, Melville forces us to think otherwise. This is not because of any mystical assumption of a reality that transcends truth but because of a dread that he experiences in the face of a reality he cannot comprehend. Our understanding gives us only the surfaces and not the depths of reality. We are protected from the incursion of reality, but this means that we are protected from the full truth.

In the middle sections of *Moby Dick* we see a growing intensity of the revelation of evil as the heart of reality, and good as the appearance that first obscures and overlays evil and later on is stripped aside, as it were, so that the evil is laid bare. If Melville could no longer believe, with the sunken-eyed young Platonist of his "Masthead" chapter, that man is a microcosm of the macrocosm—a being with a secure place in the cosmos—this much at least of his transcendentalism he could retain: a correspondence between the inner world and the outer. "Some certain significance lurks in all things," says Ishmael in "The Doubloon" (XCIX), "else all things are little worth, and the round world itself but an empty cipher!" Every single thing which Ishmael says about the whale, down to the minutest details, he can also use as a symbol of the inner life of man, or the soul of man, or the destiny of man. This certainly implies no universal soul, or "Oversoul," that makes man safe in nature, no monism of truth and reality. Yet at least one last link, or thread, still exists between truth and reality, for we can in some sense know reality. We can encounter infinity even if we cannot paint it, even if we realize that it is hostile to us and will destroy us.

In "Brit" (LVIII) the whole symbolism of land and sea undergoes a complete reversal and becomes the contrast between good and evil, innocence and experience, appearance and reality. The sea, at first, has the appearance of good, but when we look beneath the surface beauty we discover that the sea is a savage, murderous, cannibalistic force. The beauty of the sea makes all the more horrible the horrors that we subsequently discover. Now the sea stands for an element essentially antithetical to man and hostile to human existence.

> For as this appalling ocean surrounds the verdant land, so in the soul of man there lies one insular Tahiti, full of peace and joy, but encompassed by all the horrors of the half known life. God keep thee! Push not off from that isle, thou canst never return!

That "insular Tahiti" is the South Seas paradise which Melville contrasted in his earlier works with the modern civilization that he did not like. It is also the "Tahiti" which every one of us experiences in the original innocence of childhood and loses forever as we cast off into a world of experience. It is perhaps, too, an almost mystic center of inward joy and peace that some souls can carry a little way intact into the world of experience. When confronted with the dark horror outside, however, or when confronting the dark horror within, it is soon irretrievably lost: one can return to it only in reminiscence, but never in reality.

It is the diabolism of the natural world that makes "truth" so inhuman, so impossible for man to bear. Melville extends the cannibalism of the sea to the cannibalism of men, producing a picture of "a shocking, sharkish" world all around. This is no longer the pantheism of the young Platonist who saw man and nature as at one with God, but a pantheism of universal, diabolical, demonic evil. Evil is not only real; it is a fully alive, universal, all-encompassing reality. What sort of a god *could* create this evil world? To quote again from Blake, "Did he who made the Lamb make thee?" when "thee" is no longer even a dreadful yet symmetrical tiger but these voracious, horrible sharks—and voracious, horrible man?

The ultimate terror, to Ishmael, is the indifference of an absolute that excludes man: "Is it that by its indefiniteness," Ishmael asks, that whiteness "shadows forth the heartless voids and immensities of the universe, and thus stabs us from behind with the thought of annihilation, when beholding the white depths of the milky way?" Now indefiniteness is not a characteristic of truth but of an irrational force that threatens us with annihilation—that purely quantitative infinite of sheer nonlimitation that has no respect for human limitations. Here we have evil in its second major form of indifference, an evil as terrible as or more terrible than the first form of intelligible malignity. In the end these two types of evil fuse in such a way that *Moby Dick* receives the full cumulative force of both: the inscrutability of the malignant whale joins with the indifference of the infinite universe; while the hostile whale comes toward the sailor and tears him to bits, the sun and the sea smile on indifferently "as at a birth or bridal."

There is, however, an important difference between these two types of evil, symbolized by Ahab's concentration on Moby Dick himself and Ishmael's concentration on the whiteness of his hump. In Ahab all evil focuses *in* to Moby Dick. In Ishmael the whiteness of the whale points *out* to the whole universe. Ishmael can tolerate diffuse anxiety and Ahab cannot. In the language of modern psychiatry, Ahab is analogous to the paranoiac, Ishmael the neurotic. Ahab personalizes all evil—for him even the intangible is malignant. Ishmael depersonalizes it; behind the universe there is, perhaps, not an evil god but a heartless and indifferent void. While Ahab has a more terrible aloneness and isolation from other men than Ishmael, his belief that in attacking Moby Dick he is rebelling against the evil that torments him makes his exile less profound than that of Ishmael, who cannot come up against, much less hate, the indifferent evil that oppresses him.

"All visible objects, man, are but as pasteboard masks," says Ahab to his first mate Starbuck. "In each event—in the living act, the undoubted deed—there, some unknown, but still reasoning thing puts forth the mouldings of its features from behind the unreasoning mask." The horror that this "little lower layer" opens to Ahab is that what seems irrational is really rational yet unknowable, that it is both inscrutable and malicious. "Inscrutable malice" brings together two meanings of evil that are played on again and again in the course of *Moby Dick*: on the one hand, the personal malignancy that lies behind the seemingly impersonal or ordinary natural reality; on the other hand, the impersonal, and therefore the inhuman and antihuman, reality that confronts us in the world if we see it as it is. The only thing one can do in the face of this hostile reality is to strike out at it. Ahab feels himself suffocated by this mask "shoved near" to him; the only way he can live is to break through it and destroy it. "That inscrutable thing is chiefly what I hate; and be the white whale agent, or be the white whale principal, I will wreak that hate upon him."

What particularly invests the White Whale with terror is "that unexampled, intelligent malignity which . . . he had over and over again evinced in his assaults." Ishmael in no way suggests that "that intangible malignity" itself exists only in the mind of Ahab or that it is a merely psychological phenomenon. On the contrary, "it has been from the beginning," and even the modern Christian, like the ancient Gnostic, sees that evil as at least as powerful as good, and probably more powerful. The Gnostic Ophites drew the logical conclusion that it is the devil, or snake, that should be worshiped and propitiated, not God. We do not find here, as in Zoroastrianism, the almost equal conflict of good and evil, with good bound to win out in the end with the aid of the free and rational decision of man. Rather, as in Gnosticism, evil is radically real, more real, in fact, than good on the plane of this world.

Ahab's ship the *Pequod* is a little world that, like the great one, has neither meaning nor purpose, as, like some gigantic horse, it bears its burning freight into the night. The picture of the ship driven by furies to a relentless doom and the implicit suggestion that this is also the ship of the world "on its passage out" is reinforced by the impression uppermost in Ishmael's mind as he stands at the helm, "that whatever swift, rushing thing I stood on was not so much bound to any haven ahead as rushing from all havens astern." The unsurpassable image of chaos that these passages afford suggests not only the diabolism of the ancient Gnostics but also modern man's sense of the earth hurtling through the empty space of the heavens on its meaningless progress toward extinction. Even the sentence that seems to imply a purpose to the voyage— "The burning ship drove on, as if remorselessly commissioned to some vengeful deed"—actually gives us a foreboding of the predestined end of Ahab's quest and hints at the chaos that is at the core of his cosmos. Somewhere between the foolish optimist and the too-wise madman, Ishmael, and without question Melville, too,

92

hoped to find the truly wise man who could face the evil and suffering of the world without being overwhelmed by it. To be truly human, one must have the wisdom that is woe. Yet one has to stop short of immersing oneself in that woe, stop short of madness. One cannot prove oneself human through the attitude of a "jolly Stubb," the second mate who grins at Moby Dick and will not take him seriously. But neither can one authenticate oneself in the way of Ahab, who, like an inverted idealist, turns the natural rebellion of the whale against being killed into a universal, metaphysical evil, who captures the crew within his own inner world and his own purpose, and who refuses, even on encountering other ships, to recognize any reality other than that of his monomaniac hunt.

If the fire is artificial, the ocean is all too real, and the same sun which disperses the night and all false lamps can only light up, not hide, this dark two-thirds of the earth. To face reality means to recognize the predominance of evil and suffering: "That mortal man who hath more of joy than sorrow in him . . . cannot be true, not true, or undeveloped."[1]

6

Human Demonism

Black Elk and *Rabbit Boss*

In this chapter we turn from natural to human evil. Most of the encounter with evil that we have followed in *Moby Dick* has been that with nature and, by implication, a metaphysical evil that undergirds creation. We have touched only tangentially on Melville's superb portrayal of the way in which Captain Ahab, through pitting himself against the evil of Moby Dick, becomes evil himself—impersonal, monological, unfree, and even inhuman. Human evil is dealt with more centrally in Melville's novel *The Confidence Man* where the correlation is made between mistrust of man (misanthropy) and mistrust of the Creator (infidelity).

The evil that the Native American has responded to is above all that brought by the white man. More important than individual acts and even the decimation of the Native American race has been the total destruction of their world. At one point when Black

Elk is singing a ceremonial song, "all the people began to weep together because the Wasichus [the whitemen] had taken the beautiful world away from us."

The Native American's encounter with evil is beautifully depicted in the last chapter of the epic novel *Rabbit Boss* in the speech of "Christ"—a Paiute Indian:

> Where the Whiteman walks the Buffalo Bulls no longer walk. Where the Whiteman walks the rivers run dry and the trees fall. Where the Whiteman walks men turn their hearts against one another. The days are falling. We are sick with a white swelling. We spit the blasted blood of our hearts on a land gone lame with murderous grace. *They* have locked us off the land. The land is the heart. To lose touch with the land is to lose touch with the heart. . . .
>
> Now the songs are lost. The dances dead, the fires grown cold, the ceremonies swallowed up. The White bullets went through the hearts at Wounded Knee and the hearts thrown in a hole to be buried in frozen Earth. . . . It is the Whiteman who killed our collecting grounds . . . cutting the roots of all green growing from Earth until the Antelope were dead . . . the Buffalo were dead, the Deer were dead. . . . The Whiteman yanked the silver and gold veins from the Earth and killed the trees. . . . He made us betray our Brothers. The Whiteman gave us a dream of hate. . . .[2]

Even more than in *Black Elk Speaks* the final cry is a cry of despair:

> All the dreams are dead. The people are dead or dying. Their Spirits rot in a land sunk to the heart. . . . We are as empty as the day Coyote molded the Earth. There is no power for tomorrow. Tomorrow will kill us because we cannot go out to meet it.[3]

Toni Morrison's *Beloved*

The evil which the African-American has encountered has been, of course, four hundred years of slavery and its aftereffects, including not only continued economic hardship and discrimination, but also conflicts within the structure of African-American families.

Toni Morrison's novel *Beloved* is a modern masterpiece which takes one's breath away both through the originality of its form and the effectiveness with which that original project is carried out. Although there is much explicit concern with religion in the part of the novel where Baby Suggs, the grandmother, preaches in the woods outside of Cincinnati in open-air meetings, the deepest religious attitude and theme of the book is connected with "Beloved," the two-year old child killed by its mother, Sethe, when the men from Kentucky come with the sheriff to take Sethe and her family back to slavery. In the first part of the novel Beloved is present as a rambunctious ghost, but after she is driven out by Paul D., one of the "Sweet Home" boys who has reconnected with Sethe after twenty years and tries to live with her, Beloved returns as a young, embodied woman of the very age that she would have been had she not been killed. Her younger sister Denver knows this immediately, and in due time her mother realizes it herself. But this is only after Paul D. has been driven out by Beloved and by the newspaper clipping that informs him of how Sethe tried to kill all her children and did actually kill one rather than see them return to slavery.

The plot of the novel, in so far as there is one, is entirely focused on the interaction of Baby Suggs (while she is alive), Sethe, Denver, Beloved, and Paul D., with many flashbacks to the horrendous experiences most of them have had in the past parts of their lives. This is all done with such masterful interweaving of past and present that nowhere does the reader's interest flag or the credibility of the novel waver. The burden of the novel is a powerful plaint on the part of the African-American against the inhumanity of the whites toward their black slaves and the blacks who were not slaves, and with it the recognition of the truncated humanity of those whites themselves.

The way that this is done is at once powerful and subtle, with faithful attention to all the details of the maiming of Baby Suggs, the "tree" that appears on Sethe's back as a result of her rape and beating at Sweet Home, the subjection of Paul D. to wearing a bit in his mouth like a horse, and the murder of Halle's mind when he watches from above what is being done to his wife, Sethe.

After Sethe's violent response to her near recaptivity, Baby Suggs gives up her preaching and retires to her bed, studying colors one by one in order "to fix on something harmless in the world." She refuses to be called back to her religious task by Stamp Paid, who claims she has to be there for others: "Can't nobody Call like you." Now, years later, when he is trying in vain to get into the house where Sethe, Denver, and Beloved live, in order to make up for his having driven Paul D. away by showing him the old clipping, Stamp Paid regrets that conversation:

> the high tone he took; his refusal to see the effect of marrow weariness in a woman he believed was a mountain. Now, too late, he understood her. The heart that pumped out love, the mouth that spoke the Word, didn't count. They came in her yard anyway and she could not approve or condemn Sethe's rough choice. One or the other might have saved her, but beaten up by the claims of both, she went to bed. The whitefolks had tired her out at last.

And him. Eighteen seventy-four and whitefolks were still on the loose. Whole towns wiped clean of Negroes; eighty-seven lynchings in one year alone in Kentucky; four colored schools burned to the ground; grown men whipped like children; children whipped like adults; black women raped by the crew; property taken, necks broken. He smelled skin, skin and hot blood. The skin was one thing, but human blood cooked in a lynch fire was a whole other thing.[4]

Even these things had not worn out Stamp Paid's marrow. But finding at the bottom of the river a red ribbon knotted around a curl of wet woolly hair, clinging still to its bit of scalp, did. "What *are* these people?" he exclaims to the frozen mud of the road and the river beyond. "You tell me, Jesus. What *are* they?"

Primo Levi

Primo Levi is the Italian survivor of Auschwitz who wrote several remarkable books on his experience, foremost among them *Survival in Auschwitz.* This work fell into oblivion after its modest publication in 1947 and achieved new life only with its republication in 1958, after which a half million copies were sold in Italy alone and the book was translated into eight languages.

In this book we are told that the newcomers to Auschwitz experienced the first meeting with those who were already inmates of the *Lager,* or camp, as "incomprehensible and mad," but also as what they themselves would be transformed into tomorrow. "Today, in our times, hell must be like this," the author concludes after his first day in camp when they are indeed "transformed" into creatures who have reached the bottom:

> No human condition is more miserable than this, nor could it conceivably be so. Nothing belongs to us anymore; they have taken away our clothes, our shoes, even our hair; if we speak, they will not listen to us, and if they listen, they will not understand.[5]

Forgetful of dignity and restraint, the inmates have been transformed into people "whose life or death can be lightly decided with no sense of human affinity." This is the double meaning of the term extermination camp. "In this place everything is forbidden, not for hidden reasons, but because the camp has been created for that purpose."

The hell into which they have descended is not only absurd, it is evil. Everything is hostile and malevolent around them; the very barbed wire that separates them from the world is felt as an evil presence. And on the scaffolding, trains, roads, and in the pits and offices there are only slaves and masters, the masters slaves themselves, all motivated by fear and hatred, all enemies or rivals. Everyone is killed in spirit long before his or her anonymous death; no one may leave to carry to the world "the evil tidings of what man's presumption made of man in Auschwitz."

And at nighttime the hunger, blows, cold, exhaustion, and fear of the days turns into "shapeless nightmares of unheard-of violence" from which one wakes up at every moment, frozen with terror, shaking in every limb—"a sorrowful turmoil in which we all feel ourselves trapped and suffocated . . . marching in a circle, without beginning or end, with a blinding giddiness and a sea of nausea rising from the praecordia to the gullet."

Nothing of the ordinary moral world survives inside the barbed wire since thief and victim are punished with equal gravity. "Good" and "evil," "just" and "unjust" no longer have any meaning. The only meaningful categories are that of the saved and the drowned. In the *Lager* the struggle to survive is without respite since "everyone is desperately and ferociously alone," engulfed and swept along without rest by the innumerable crowd, yet encased in an opaque intimate solitude in which "they die or disappear, without leaving a trace in anyone's memory." The drowned are the *Musselmänner,* non-men who march and labor in silence, too empty to suffer, too dead to really die. The *Musselman,* emaciated, head dropped, shoulders curved, face and eyes empty of every trace of thought, becomes for Levi the one image that might enclose all the evil of our time.

The "saved," in contrast, are often "prominents," Jewish and non-Jewish alike, who viciously and sadistically oppress those beneath them. Those who accept a position of privilege by betraying their natural solidarity with their comrades become hateful and hated, cruel and tyrannical, directing at the oppressed all the hatred that they dare not direct at the oppressors. Although the evidence of this cruel hierarchy is particularly evident in the *Lager,* Levi claims it as a general law that an analogous position of rivalry and hatred among the subjected has been brought about in our days in whatever country a foreign people have set foot as invaders. But the "saved" also included those prisoners who fought by every means to survive, throttling all dignity, killing all conscience, and climbing down into the arena as a beast against other beasts. This is a commentary not on universal human nature, but on what is the general rule: "Survival without renunciation of any part of one's own moral world . . . was conceded only to very few superior individuals, made of the stuff of martyrs and saints." Otherwise the best survivor is the one who outside the camp would be a criminal and/or a madman.

Levi's picture of time in the *Lager* is remarkably similar to that which the phenomenological psychiatrist Eugene Minkowski has portrayed in a case of schizophrenic depression:

> For living men, the units of time always have a value, which increases in ratio to the strength of the internal resources of the person living through them; but for us, hours, days, months spilled out sluggishly from the future into the past, always too slowly, a valueless and superfluous material . . . the future stood in front of us, grey and inarticulate, like an invincible barrier. For us, history had stopped.[6]

In his book *Moments of Reprieve* Levi narrates stories that are the exception rather than the rule. Yet he ends with a story that is the most exceptional of all—the fantastic saga of Chaim Rumkowski, the self-inflated Jewish "emperor" of the Nazi ghetto of Lodz, Poland—and makes it into a mirror for human nature in general. We are all ambiguous hybrids of clay and spirit. Rumkowski's "miserable tinsel trappings" are "the distorted image of our symbols of social prestige." Like Rumkowski, says Levi,

> we too are so dazzled by power and money as to forget our essential fragility, forget that all of us are in the ghetto, that the ghetto is fenced in, that beyond the fence stand the lords of death, and not far away the train is waiting.[7]

Much in the spirit of this statement is Levi's 1946 poem "Shema," which changes the injunction of Deuteronomy to tell the words of God to one's children into a curse on those who live secure in warm houses and return at evening to find hot food and friendly faces if they do not consider at every moment whether the man and woman in the death camp who fights for a crust of bread and dies at a yes or no is really a human being. "May their house crumble, disease render them powerless, and their offspring avert their faces from them!" cries out the poet. For Adolf Eichmann, "son of death," the poet does not wish death but five million sleepless nights in which he is visited each night by the suffering of those who were shut into the gas chambers "air filled with death." Even as late as 1981 in a poem celebrating "The Partisan," Levi pictures every man as the enemy of every other and split by an inner border: "On your feet, old men, enemies of yourselves, our war is never over." And the 1984 poem "The Elephant" Levi ends with the words "Absurd, absurd."[8]

Levi takes the title of his last (1986) book, *The Drowned and the Saved,* from a chapter of *Survival in Auschwitz,* next to which it is his most important book for our purposes. Both victims and oppressors had a keen awareness of the enormity and noncredibility of what took place in the *Lagers.* Fully aware of all the terrible events that have taken place in the world since Auschwitz, Levi nonetheless declares the Nazi concentration camp system a *unicum* both in its extent and its quality: "Never have so many human lives been extinguished in so short a time, and with so lucid a combination of technological ingenuity, fanaticism, and cruelty." What is more, time does not heal the injury. The tormentor remains tormented, and the abomination of the annihilation is never extinguished.

In the chapter on "The Gray Zone" Levi considers how unfair privilege appears in all human coexistence, and the war against it is endless. The harsher the oppression, the more widespread among the oppressed is the willingness to collaborate—because of terror, ideological seduction, servile imitation of the victor, or greedy desire for even the most trivial power. The most extreme example of "privilege" were the *Sonderkommandos,* the special death squads who ran the crematoria for a few months until they in turn were gassed and cremated. "Conceiving and organizing the squads was National Socialism's most demonic crime," writes Levi. Let us meditate on the story of these "crematorium ravens" with pity and rigor but without judging them, he requests. Martin Buber writes that one can only know one's resources by using them. In similar, starker vein, Levi writes:

> Nobody can know for how long and under what trials his soul can resist before yielding or breaking. Every human being possesses a reserve of strength whose extent is unknown to him, be it large, small, or nonexistent, and only through extreme adversity can we evaluate it.[9]

In chapter 3 on "Shame" Levi points out that for most the hour of liberation was neither joyful nor lighthearted but anguished, for with it returned not only their sorrow but also their responsibility and their shame. Those survivors who deliberately damaged, robbed, or beat their companions could block out the memory, but "almost everybody feels guilty of having omitted to offer help" to the needy companions at their side. "There was no time, space, privacy, patience, strength; most often, the person to whom the request was addressed found himself in his turn in a state of need, entitled to comfort."

Everyone suffered from a nameless, unceasing discomfort that polluted sleep—"the anguish . . . of a deserted and empty universe . . . from which the spirit of man is absent." Levi knew exactly from firsthand experience what Buber meant by defining existential guilt not only as guilt that one has taken on oneself as a person, but also as guilt that comes with the injury of the common order the foundations of which one recognizes, at some level, as the foundation of one's own and of all human existence. Denied the screen of willed ignorance, not able not to see the ocean of pain that surrounded and submerged them, the just

104

among the prisoners felt remorse, shame, and pain even for the misdeeds that others had created—the infinite enormity of pain which could never be cleansed: the "shame of the world."

Levi stresses again and again that the survivors are not the true witnesses because those who touched bottom did not return. Like Viktor Frankl, Levi declares that the best did not survive and adds: "Probably the worst survived, the selfish, the violent, the insensitive, the collaborators of the 'gray zone,' the spies." Even though Levi personally felt innocent, as one of the survivors he felt in permanent search of justification in his own eyes and those of others.

Only the deposition of the *Musselmänner* would have had general significance. But even if the drowned, i.e., those who touched bottom and did not survive, had paper and pen, they would not have testified because their death had begun before the death of their body: "They had already lost the ability to observe, to remember, to compare and express themselves. We speak in their stead, by proxy."

A part of the death and dehumanization of the inmates lay in the destruction of that communicating which makes the human being human: "For those people [i.e., their captors] we were no longer men. With us, as with cows or mules, there was no substantial difference between a scream and a punch." As a result almost everyone drowned in a stormy sea of not-understanding, receiving slaps and kicks without comprehending why. "Where violence is inflicted on man it is also inflicted on language."

Reading the systematic consideration of successive themes in *The Drowned and the Saved,* one can understand how even some of those who were never in extermination camps have been led to commit suicide after immersing themselves in the literature of the *Shoah.* One of the most painful of these chapters is that on "Useless Violence." The useless cruelty of violated modesty which conditioned the existence of all the *Lagers* is only paradigmatic of innumerable examples:

One is truly led to think that, in the Third Reich, the best choice, the choice imposed from above, was the one that entailed the greatest affliction, the greatest waste, the greatest physical and moral suffering. The "enemy" must not only die, he must die in torment.[10]

Levi espies one use for all this useless violence, namely that before dying the victim must be degraded, so that the murderer will be less burdened by guilt. Though not devoid of logic, this explanation "shouts to heaven."

A popular saying during the Second World War was that there were no atheists in foxholes. Levi, experiencing unimaginably worse than any foxhole, entered and left the *Lager* as a nonbeliever, confirmed in this nonbelief by an experience that made it impossible for him to conceive any form of providence or transcendent justice: "Why were the moribund packed in cattle cars? Why were the children sent to the gas?" Even Elie Wiesel says that after the *Shoah* those who do *not* rebel and express anger against God have no real faith.[11]

Toward the end of *The Drowned and the Saved* Levi quotes Norberto Bobbio: "the Nazi extermination camps were . . . not *one of the* events, but *the* monstrous, perhaps unrepeatable event of human history. . . ." We owe to survivors like Primo Levi and Elie Wiesel such awareness of that event as we are able to imagine and make our own.

Part Three

Holding the Tension between Affirming and Withstanding

7

Kafka and Kundera: Two Voices from Prague

Franz Kafka's *Castle*: The Calling and the Call

In a comment on my book *Problematic Rebel: Melville, Dostoievsky, Kafka, Camus*, Martin Buber wrote:

> The theme is the revolt of man against an existence emptied of meaning, the existence after the so-called "death of God." . . . One must withstand this meaninglessness, must suffer it to the end, must do battle with it undauntedly, until out of the contradiction experienced in conflict and suffering, meaning shines forth anew.

The destruction of meaning in the particular through the encounter with evil has placed us squarely before the absurd. After this encounter meaning is to be recovered, not through a retreat to the innocent immediacy of the particular and still less through a fall-

109

back to some general worldview or overall design from the perspective of which the evil of the particular is to be affirmed. It can only be recovered by going through and beyond the absurd to the place where one can hold the tension between affirming where one can affirm and withstanding where one must withstand. As a result, meaning and the absurd are left in tension with each other.

No one puts this tension before us so honestly and compellingly as Franz Kafka (1883-1924). In every line that he has written, whether in finished stories, unfinished novels, notations in his diary, or letters, this is his central concern. To say this is not to dismiss the wealth of aspects and levels in Kafka's writings which have received so much attention from his interpreters. Rather, it is to indicate the wholeness that gives his work its central significance.

If concern for human existence in its concrete reality makes one an "existentialist," then Kafka is more of an existentialist than most of those who today are called by this name. He does not start with any absolute or with the assumption of the death of God, but with human existence itself. Those who seek to understand and interpret Kafka through some allegorical key, whether religious, psychoanalytic, or sociological, miss the simple fact that, paradoxical as it is, Kafka's world is not a transparent one through which we can glimpse some other, more familiar reality. It is just what it is in its irreducible opaqueness and absurdity. "The only really difficult and insoluble problems are those which we cannot formulate," writes Kafka, "because they have the difficulties of life itself as their content." Kafka, however, is not a philosopher but an artist. His writing cannot be reduced to abstract philosophical concepts any more than it can be reduced to religious or political allegories, mystical symbols, or psychoanalytic case histories. Yet his stories and novels have a curiously abstract quality. Kafka's heroes are never full-dimensional, concrete human beings, and his stories never have the ring of everyday reality, no matter how detailed and circumstantial they may be.

The key to Kafka, perhaps, is that sense of caricature which is borne in on us again and again. If one feels that one recognizes reality in Kafka, one always feels at the same time that it is a reality that is somehow caricatured. Though this caricature is of the nature of an abstraction from concrete reality, it does not point outward to some still more abstract concept but back to an altogether concrete way of seeing—a perception of reality that again and again lays bare the absurdity inherent in Kafka's particular relationship to it, if not in reality itself. Kafka's stories do not suggest a really open response to the unique reality of person and situation such as we find again and again in Dostoyevsky. In Kafka, as a result, the romantic grandeur of Melville and the profound realism of Dostoyevsky are replaced by an almost ascetic restriction in subject matter and perspective that makes his creations more thoroughly unromantic, unheroic, and nonpathetic than even the most "realistic" and sordid of portrayals.

Kafka's heroes move from self-sufficiency to ever more anxious isolation and exile. Some of them experience the world's breaking in on the self, destroying its security and calling it to account. Others are engaged in a hopeless and unceasing striving for a contact with reality that they can never attain, a call that they can never clearly hear, and an uncertain calling that will "answer" that call. The result is guilt and anxiety. The conclusion is that there is a goal, but there is no way; the "way" is only a hesitation or wavering. "The true way goes over a rope which is not stretched at any great height but just above the ground," reads a Kafka aphorism. "It seems more designed to make people stumble than to be walked upon."

As important as the question of Joseph K.'s guilt in *The Trial,* is the frighteningly irregular and corrupt bureaucracy that has him in its clutches. This bureaucracy wraps its tentacles around the whole of Joseph K.'s reality until it finally crushes him to death—with his compliance. Most of the workings of the Law are removed from sight and understanding, while what can be seen offers a spectacle of disgusting dirt and disorder. The goddess of Justice is portrayed by the court painter as "a goddess of the Hunt in full cry." K. accepts his guilt in the end and reaches out at the same time for help. Yet neither of these attitudes saves him from dying grotesquely and cruelly, "like a dog!" All this may seem simply absurd, yet if we put it together with the problem of existential guilt that lies at the heart of *The Trial*, we discover that what Kafka is really pointing to is what I call in my books on the human image the "Dialogue with the Absurd." This is a position which I see developed in both Kafka and Camus. "Everything is not summed up in negation and absurdity," says Camus in *The Rebel*. "But we must first posit negation and absurdity because they are what our generation has encountered and what we must take into account." Camus moves to and Kafka, for all his negation, stands at the position that in *Problematic Rebel* I have called the Modern Job—the person whose contending still includes the trust that meaning may be found in the Dialogue with the Absurd.

In *The Trial*, Kafka is clearly as concerned about the grotesque absurdity of the world that K. encounters as about K.'s existential guilt. But he is concerned most of all about the confrontation of these two, about what happens when the world breaks in on the self as it does on K. Although the world that confronts the self is absurd, it places a real demand on the self that the latter must meet. The self can find meaning in its existence neither through rationalizing away the absurdity of the world nor through rejecting the world's demand because of this absurdity, but through answering with its existence the demand that comes to it through the absurd and that can reach it in no other way.

Kafka's last and greatest novel, *The Castle,* is the story of the attempt of K., "a disreputable-looking man in his thirties," to get some foothold in the village which he has just entered as a total stranger and to make some contact with the Castle which stands above the village. Though K. at first glance seems to be the lone exile in a community of secure and settled villagers, it becomes clear that the villagers, too, are in exile at the very place where it seems most unthinkable, namely, in their relation to the Castle. The mutual distrust which exists between the villagers and the Castle officials belies the assertion that there is no gulf between them and nothing to be bridged. Despite all this, practically everyone in the village has a childlike trust or dogmatic faith in the officials that rules out categorically all possibility of error and evil on their part. The Castle official is presumed to be right, even when he seems wrong, while the villager must presume himself wrong even when he seems right.

K. looks on the Castle as happy and free in itself but as threatening and cruel in its relations with him. K.'s relation to particular officials tends to follow a pattern of hope followed by disappointment, ending finally in indifference. Above all, K. seems to be prevented from getting anywhere in his own suit because of his impatience. Yet his impatience is the result of his anxiety—the anxiety of the exile and the stranger who has no sure ground on which to stand. Even if there were such a thing as a "true way," K. could not find it, or if he found it, he could not follow it. He does not have any access to immediate existence that would make it possible for him to live the moment for itself or relate to another person for the sake of the relationship alone. Throughout the novel, K. remains in transition, while trying in vain to leave this condition by every means possible.

K. is constantly assured from all sides that he was not called and not needed and that his "calling" is no real "calling." He is left to establish his calling himself, yet this is exactly what he cannot do. Before he can be accepted in the village, and still more important, before he can begin his work as Land-Surveyor, he needs the confirmation of the Castle—a confirmation which he never receives in any unequivocal or really effective way. What we have here, therefore, is a sort of inverted calling—the need to be called coupled with the impossibility of proving that one is called and the improbability that anyone else will prove it for one.

If K. needs a call to confirm his calling, he also uses his "calling" as a way of answering whatever it is in this "desolate country" that has called him and that makes him want to stay. Whatever this call is, it does not come from other people, no matter how much K. gets himself involved with them in the course of the novel. He sees people as a means to the end of contacting the Castle or as a trap to sidetrack him and prevent his reaching it. He hardly ever sees his relationship to others as a value in itself.

Kafka could live only as a writer, not because he wished to escape from life, but because in his writing alone could he find meaning in his existence and *understand* the meaning of his existence. In partial analogy to this, K.'s calling as Land-Surveyor makes him a person who seeks, in one way or another, to find, understand, and respond to meaning, and the meaning that he finds is not some essence of existence but concrete existence itself, the irreducible "given." An in-depth study of *The Castle* suggests that K.'s calling as Land-Surveyor is already in the deepest sense a seeking to answer a call—the call of existence itself. K. wants some assurance that he is not *merely* presuming (Erich Heller points out that the German meaning of *vermessen*, the verb from which *Vermesser* [Land-Surveyor] derives, is 'to presume'), that he has the right to separate himself from the calling of ordinary people and take on the unique task of finding and defining meaning.

K. does not look on the Castle as the means to living in the village, as Max Brod suggested; the village, rather, is the means to reaching the Castle. Social reality is either a means or an obstacle for K. It is not a goal. K.'s call is not a call to life in relation to people. It is a call to a unique and lonely relation to the Castle. But for all K.'s desire to bypass the village and reach the Castle directly, he never does so and, in the nature of things, never can.

Kafka's world differs from Kierkegaard's on the most essential point of all, namely Kierkegaard's belief that it is possible for the Single One to say "Thou" to God without saying "Thou" to man. Despite his aphorisms about the eternal and the indestructible, Kafka knows no ultimate reality that can be reached apart from the world.

If we may apply this insight to *The Castle* (from my interpretation from which it was, in fact, derived[1]), the tension between the self and the social is complemented by the tension between social reality and ultimate reality. This border realm of the social may offer us a key to K.'s problematic. Through this double tension we can understand K.'s alternation between stubborn rejection of all mediating social forms and his clinging to even the smallest social connections with the Castle. Ordinary social life is fundamentally boring to K., as it was to Kafka, yet only through some connection with the social can he hope to reach his goal. His goal, however, always remains unclear, both in itself and as to the way of reaching it, and this is because his goal is neither the village nor the Castle, but an immediacy from which he is excluded in the former and which he tries in vain to reach through the latter. Again: "There is a goal, but no way: what we call the way is only hesitation."

To sum up, K. has to prove that he has been called by the Castle to be a Land-Surveyor before he can practice his calling and survey the land. To do this he must make contact with the Castle, which he cannot do. The paradox of his calling is that he can never know who calls or how to answer, yet he must establish his calling in order to exist as a person and is accountable for the inauthenticity of his personal existence if he does not. Confronted by an absurd reality which seems by its very nature to offer no personal meaning, he is, nonetheless, not free to run away to any "higher" reality or to abandon his search as hopeless.

In *The Castle* the social is an amorphous realm between the self and the call, a neutral strip, or "no man's land," whose borders on either side are constantly fluctuating. The fluctuation of these borders constitutes the central problematic of *The Castle*. The problem of the calling, as we have seen, is not merely that a calling is only meaningful as a response to a call and that a call is needed to confirm the calling, but also that the confirmation needs to be personal as well as social, social as well as personal. The impossibility of identifying social and personal confirmation, on the one hand, and of separating them, on the other, is paradigmatic of the whole situation of the self. K. is a masterful portrayal of the confusion of the anxious and at the same time reflective person who fights for freedom and independence, yet recognizes both the necessity of social binding and the extent to which one is not so much an individual as a social unit.

The other border is between the social and the ultimate reality—what we might call "ontological reality" in order to distinguish it in some way from the social without erecting it into a separate metaphysical or theological realm. Here, too, the self experiences great confusion, this time from the side of the call. The call seems to come through the social, yet in such a way that it not only becomes indistinct but often highly dubious. It tempts one to believe, as a result, either that there really is no call or that it comes to one from some metaphysical, religious, or eternal realm quite outside the social. The problematic of the social, as a result, becomes essential to understanding both the self and the call.

116

In the world of *The Castle* the self finds meaning not through identifying society and social confirmation with the call nor through turning away from them to some pure call that one hears apart from the world. It finds meaning, rather, through answering with its existence the call that comes to it through the absurd— through the bigoted villagers and the endless, senseless hierarchies of Castle officials, the call that can reach it in no other way. K. never sees any "ultimate reality," he never hears the call except as it is mediated through social reality. He hears the call in such a way, what is more, that he can neither separate social and ultimate reality on the one hand, nor accept social reality as simply reality on the other.

K. is in some respects a Modern Job, if a lesser and less passionate one. Like Job, K. demands direct contact with ultimate reality. As Job is not content just to hear about God but wants to see God face to face, so K. is not content with Klamm's environment: he wants to see Klamm face to face and go beyond Klamm into the Castle. Like Job, K. does not feel impelled to choose between the self and what transcends it. "He may well slay me. I am ready to accept it," says Job. "Yet I shall argue my ways before His face." Although K. recognizes that he may not be able to face Klamm, this is no reason for refraining from the attempt. "If I only succeed in holding my ground, . . . I shall at any rate have the satisfaction of having spoken my mind freely to a great man." Like Job, too, K. contends. "I am here to fight," he says in the variant of the opening. Like Job, K. dares what others do not and is condemned by the upholders of tradition as proud and presumptuous. Although "he had arrived yesterday, and the Castle had been here since ancient times," K. demands what Job demands and what every person alive has the right to demand—the opportunity to confront the Castle directly and with the whole of one's existence. In so far as he stands his ground and contends, K. is like Kafka himself. To Kafka, our task is not to escape from the absurd into inward contemplation but to stand and withstand, to hear and contend. Kafka fights against the transience of the world, not by leaving the world for some immutable, metaphysical realm but through perceiving and creating, hoping and despairing. Kafka discovers the human again and again, in the very heart of the bewildering social hierarchy, personal meaning in the midst of the impersonal absurd. Kafka possesses a trust in existence which not all the terror and conflict of his life can destroy. It is a trust that the world will come to you unsummoned. But it is no less a trust that the world calls you and that you can call the world. Life's splendor lies forever in wait, writes Kafka, veiled but not hostile, reluctant, or deaf. "If you summon it by the right word, by its right name, it will come."

Kafka depicted the course of the world in gloomier colors than ever before, wrote Martin Buber in *Two Types of Faith*, yet he also proclaimed trust in existence anew, "with a still deepened 'in spite of all this,' quite soft and shy, but unambiguous." Kafka's modern Kabbala stressed the exile of the soiled and suffering immanence of God from the hidden transcendence, in place of the traditional kabbalistic reunification of God and the world. Kafka offered us only this "trust in spite of"—the complaint of a Modern Job who will not give up struggling to find meaning in his suffering but who can never affirm that meaning in the unqualified fashion of the biblical Job to whom God has come near again. "So must Trust change in a time of God's eclipse in order to preserve steadfast to God, without disowning reality," comments Martin Buber, and adds, "The contradiction of existence becomes for us a theophany." Such "theophany" as Kafka experiences comes not apart from but through the very heart of "the contradiction of existence," holding the tension between affirming and withstanding.

Milan Kundera's *Immortality*: Deconstructing the Illusion of Personal Uniqueness

In one of Kafka's short sketches a man comes into the room of another man, gets out a case of knives, and starts sharpening one, announcing at the same time that he is going to execute the other man. "You can't do that," the victim protests. "There can be no execution without a hearing and a trial." "You are thinking of fairy tales," the executioner replies, "but this is no fairy tale." And he continues sharpening his knife. The beginning of the Absurd, as Camus defines it, is the expectation of a rationality which is not present. Yet further along even that expectation disappears. Ishmael in Melville's *Moby Dick* finds evil in indifference. "Is it by its indefiniteness that it shadows forth the heartless voids and immensities of the universe and thus stabs us from behind with the thought of annihilation when beholding the white depths of the milky way?" Ishmael asks. But when Meursault is about to be guillotined in Camus's novel *The Stranger,* he expects so little of the world that he speaks of "the benign indifference of the universe." For Meursault the "partnership of existence," to use my phrase, is just that benign indifference, or even, so he may feel less lonely, the shouts of hatred and contempt that will greet his execution.

Kafka, even less than Camus, expected rationality; yet moving from Kafka to the Czech novelist Milan Kundera is moving to a world where the Absurd is so much the expected that it is no longer seen as absurd. Kundera's world is not so opaque as Kafka's, yet in some ways it is even more curious. In his recent novel *Immortality* Kundera not only inserts his own philosophizings on various subjects, as in previous novels, but even enters the novel himself as author and character combined, accompanied by

119

Professor Avenarius, a friend who serves a similar bridge function. Thus the point of view does not come to us through the tensions of points of view, as in Kafka. But neither can we say with any sureness what Kundera's point of view is, despite his all too numerous authorial interventions.

Kundera wants the novel to be a form that cannot be paraphrased in any other medium, and he certainly succeeds with this one. He also wants it to be an end in itself and not a movement of plot toward some dramatic conclusion, and in this too he succeeds. Can *Immortality* be subsumed under what I have in the past, in *Problematic Rebel*, *To Deny Our Nothingness*, and *The Hidden Human Image*, called the "Dialogue with the Absurd" and what I now call "Holding the Tension between Affirming and Withstanding"? Here also we cannot be sure. All we can do is to juxtapose Kafka with Kundera as one might juxtapose the "modern" with the "postmodern." In doing this we shall certainly not be misled, for much of this novel seems to fit the spirit of deconstruction: from the attack on the connection between self and face to the attack on the uniqueness of the self, and the insistence that our gestures possess us rather than we them since there are many more people in the world than there are gestures to go around.

The book begins with the youthful gesture of an older woman at a swimming pool, a gesture witnessed by the author and one that leads him to invent the central character Agnes and, in time, her father and mother, her sister Laura, and her husband Paul. Agnes is compared on the cover to Madame Bovary and Anna Karenina, and this seems apt in light of the fact that her whole life seems to be a withdrawal from relationship with anyone but her dead father. It is, in fact, exactly what the American psychoanalyst Leslie Farber called "a life of suicide." Yet this very withdrawal places Agnes in the superior, impregnable position that leaves her husband Paul at a total loss. This is symbolized by the mysterious smile on her face after she has been killed in a truly absurd automobile accident. This smile has no reference at all to Paul, who has shown up fifteen minutes too late as a result of Professor Avenarius's absurd slashing of the tires of automobiles while he is jogging. Paul faints, but the reader holds up since, in contrast to Madame Bovary and Anna Karenina, one can see no tragedy here at all. Death was exactly what Agnes wanted, and as she lay dying she prayed that she would succeed in dying before Paul reached her, a "prayer" which is granted.

Agnes's sister Laura is of some secondary interest in her affairs with the TV announcer Bernard Bertrand (son of the legislator politician Bertrand), with Professor Avenarius, and, after Agnes's death, with Paul, whom she marries in an ultimate incestuous fulfillment of her lifelong desire to imitate, overtake, and catch up with her older sister Agnes. Laura even steals from Agnes the gesture that gave rise to the novel, after which Agnes refuses to use it herself. It is this gesture which ends Laura's part of the novel when Laura takes her farewell of Kundera, Professor Avenarius, and Paul, who are having lunch together. Although married to Paul and mother of his child, she leaves him for a long period without explanation and when she returns is hardly there for him. Paul is visibly shrinking and aging under our eyes until Laura uses Agnes's gesture, which he mistakenly sees as for himself when it is really for Professor Avenarius.

What I want to draw attention to in *Immortality*, however, is not this absurd plot but the leitmotifs with which the book abounds, either in the form of reflections of the characters or of brief authorial essays. The first of these is a thought Agnes's father shares with her when she is a child and on which she meditates after she is grown up, namely that the world is the Creator's computer. In this thought God is compared not to the deist's watchmaker who started the machine and then left it to itself nor to the traditional notion of an all-powerful God who predetermined everything, but to someone who programs a cosmic computer. "This does not mean that the future has been planned down to the last detail, that everything is written 'up above.' "[2] This image sets a realistically absurd and impersonal tone for the book which is amplified by the first actual leitmotif: the denial that there is any link between the face and the uniqueness of the self or, for that matter, that there actually is any uniqueness of the self. Agnes sees the face as an "accidental and unrepeatable combination of features" which "reflects neither character nor soul, nor what we call the self." Yet without a passionately held basic illusion that the face represents the self, we cannot live.[3]

The contemporary French philosopher Emmanuel Levinas says that it is the face of one's fellow human being, more than anything else, that presents one with the reality of otherness, of alterity, and "puts a stop to the irresistible imperialism of the same and the I." Martin Buber could not go back to Germany to give a public lecture as long as the Germans had become for him "faceless," as they did as the result of Nazism. In Part Five of his novel, on "Chance," Kundera, who consistently confuses individuality and difference with uniqueness, defines ugliness as "the poetic capriciousness of coincidence." Beauty, in contrast, comes when the "play of coincidence happens to select the average of all dimensions"—"the unpoetic average."[4]

Agnes is not unaware of the faces of Paul and her daughter Brigitte, and she even cares enough about them that she would want to know that they are alive and all right. But when the chips are down, she would not want to be reborn as the soulmate of Paul or the sister of Laura or the mother of Brigitte, and she acts this out by accepting a position in Switzerland that would have effectively removed her from all of them even if she had not been killed in the accident.

It is the memory of her father, whom she later realizes is the only person she has ever loved, that delivers Agnes from her hatred—by way of total detachment from the world: "I cannot hate them because nothing binds me to them; I have nothing in common with them." When Agnes's father is dying, he asks Agnes not to look at him anymore. Agnes obeys and lets "him leave slowly, unseen, for a world without faces." Agnes's sense of detachment goes so far that, although she knew that it was absurd and amoral, she accepted it as produced by feelings beyond her control. Actually it is the product of a growing attitude which might be described as just the opposite of Donne's famous Meditation #19 with its statement that we are a "part of the maineland." Agnes had nothing in common with these two-legged creatures with heads and mouths. Their wars and celebrations were none of her concern.[5] We cannot, of course, ascribe this point of view to Agnes's author; for if Kundera shared it, he would be incapable of writing novels.

There is one thing, we are told, that can wrench Agnes out of her attitude of "no solidarity with mankind," and that is "concrete love toward a concrete person." If she truly loved one person, she could not be indifferent to the fate of mankind since "her beloved would be dependent on that fate." But even this concrete, personal love seems to be absent from her life. She sees her love for Paul as nothing more than the will to have a happy marriage. "If she eased up on this will for just a moment, love would fly away like a bird released from its cage."[6]

In conversation with the stranger from another planet who comes at the end of Part One—"The Face"—to tell Agnes and Paul that they will not return to Earth in their next incarnation, Agnes is reassured to learn that "Faces exist nowhere else but here." In answer to the visitor's question whether they wish to remain together in the next life, "Agnes gathers all her inner strength" and answers, "'We prefer never to meet again.'" She knows that in doing so she is ruining everything between her and Paul; for this amounts to saying, "'No love ever existed between us and no love exists between us now.'" "These words are like the click of a door shutting on the illusion of love," ends Part One. What makes these deconstructions absurd is that there is no sug- gestion that the world is totally *maya,* or illusion, as in the nondu- alistic philosophy of Hinduism. Rather, like a latter-day Sartre or Camus, Kundera is left with the irrational longing for what he knows cannot be possible—uniqueness, personal meaning, love.

In Part Three—"Fighting"—"Addition and Subtraction" are set forth as a key to the two sisters and their opposite yet equally hopeless attempts to preserve their uniqueness in the face of the essential facelessness of the self. Agnes subtracts everything from herself in order to come to a sheer essence which she hopes is unique. Laura adds more and more attributes in the hope of iden- tifying with them. In *The Knowledge of Man* Buber distinguishes between the "being" person and the "seeming" person. The latter is concerned with how he or she appears to other people and tries to assume a face that will lead others to confirm him. The being person, in contrast, is able to withstand this temptation to false confirmation. He or she responds differently to different persons. However, his or her concern is not with how he or she appears but with the other person, the relationship, or the situation and the common task. By this Buber does not mean some "essence of the person" that could be distilled out of the individual as gold is mined out of ore, but the stamp of personal uniqueness on every action, utterance, and attitude. Seeming threatens the authenticity of the interhuman, according to Buber, and therefore of the human. Man's essential courage is to resist the temptation to seeming; his essential cowardice is to give in to it.

It is not surprising, given the deconstructionist reflections on the absence of personal uniqueness that we have seen above, that Kundera puts into the mouth of Paul the notion that we are all nothing but seeming persons. "As long as we live with other people, we are only what other people consider us to be." In a remarkably superficial reflection, which it would almost be embarrassing to ascribe to Kundera himself, Paul asks whether any kind of direct contact between oneself and others exists except through the eyes.[7] This, too, takes us back to Sartre with his universe of intersubjectivity based upon the way each sees others and turns them into an object (*en-soi*) or a subject (*pour-soi*) under one's own domination.

It is striking how much the above analysis is dependent upon essentially outmoded notions of "inner essence" and "outer manifestation" as the basic realities. Inner and outer, as I have written elsewhere, "are *not* primordial human reality but secondary elaborations and constructions arising from a human wholeness that precedes them both."

> The inner is psychic in the sense that we do not perceive anything with our senses, the outer physical in the sense that we do. And these divisions are useful for a certain ordering of our lives, such as the distinction between what we see, what we dream, what we envision, and what we hallucinate. . . . Yet if we think about human existence in its wholeness, we realize that a true event in our lives is neither inner nor outer but takes up and claims the whole of us. . . . Our existences interpenetrate. Inner versus outer is thus not only a distortion of the primordial human wholeness of the person, but also a distortion of the reality of our existence as person *with* person.[8]

Yet in the midst of all this denial Kundera contrasts the being in love with love, which Laura embodies, and having a real interest in the person with whom one is in love. "The emotion of love gives

125

all of us a misleading illusion of knowing the other." In *I and Thou* Buber insists that real love is not a feeling, which is at best only an accompaniment, but the responsibility of an *I* for a *Thou.* It means "knowing" the other in the full meaning of the biblical use of the term: knowing the other in mutual relationship. In his critique of Laura, Kundera understands this at least in the negative sense.

In Part Four Kundera launches an attack against feeling as *the* touchstone of reality that is quite close to Buber's critique and my own:

> *Homo sentimentalis* cannot be defined as a man with feelings (for we all have feelings), but as a man who has raised feelings to a category of value. As soon as feelings are seen as a value, everyone wants to feel; and because we all like to pride ourselves on our values, we have a tendency to show off our feelings. . . . As soon as we *want* to feel . . . , feeling is no longer feeling but an imitation of feeling, a show of feeling.[9]

Feelings are at best the accompaniment. As soon as we make them an end in itself and aim at them, as the Romantics did, they lose their reality. Yet Kundera singles out feeling as the one thing that gives any individual uniqueness, although it is a uniqueness that is not essentially dialogical, like Buber's, but is shut in itself: "The basis of the self is not thought but suffering, which is the most fundamental of all feelings. . . . In intense suffering the world disappears and each of us is alone with his self."[10]

This is a brilliant half truth. Kundera understands the unmaking of the common world that suffering and pain bring us, but not the remaking of that world that can come in what my wife, Aleene Friedman, calls "The Healing Partnership."[11]

In this same part, in one of our last glimpses of Agnes, we also

126

get a taste of an impersonal, anti-individualistic, and by implication antisocial mysticism that opts for "being" in place of "being one's self." Cleansed of the dirt of her self, Agnes participates in the "primordial being that was present even before the Creator began to create, a being that was—and still is—beyond his influence."[12] This is reminiscent of the ancient Gnostics with their distinction between the *deus absconditus*—the true God who transcends creation entirely—and the *demiurgos*—the evil God that created this evil world.

In moving from the "modern" literature of Kafka's novel *The Castle* to the "postmodern" literature of Kundera's novel *Immortality,* we have not moved closer to but further away from the Dialogue with the Absurd. While the postmodern contemporary may feel more at home in Kundera's world, there is no evidence that it combines the trust and contending of the "Modern Job" or that it holds the tension in the face of each new situation, affirming where it can affirm and withstanding where it must withstand.

8

The Harmonic, the Tragic, and the Grotesque

O ur progression in this book is a weaving between the encounter with the particular and holding the tension between affirming and withstanding. This back-and-forth progression reveals at ever deeper levels the inescapable connection between the two.

William Butler Yeats

At first glance, William Butler Yeats (1865-1939) might seem the last poet to embody the movement through and beyond the absurd to holding the tension between affirming and withstanding, since much of his life appeared to be spent on a quest for order precisely meant to deny the absurd—his Irish romanticism, mythology, and nationalism; his flirtings with the thinking of the Russian gnostic thinker Gurdjieff and theosophy; and his own occult and gnostic system, *The Vision,* which informed the first-rate poetry of his middle period with (in my judgment) second-rate philosophy. Yet there are two poems—one from his middle period and one from his late period—that do indeed embody going through and beyond the absurd.

The first of these, "The Second Coming", we have already discussed in connection with Chinua Achebe's *Things Fall Apart* since that poem is the source of the title of Achebe's novel. The second stanza of the poem is even more abrasive than the first in its encounter with the absurd, because it sets the new "revelation" that is at hand in ironic contrast with the revelation of the First Coming two thousand years ago. To the pious Christian the second coming means the appearance of Christ in power and the ushering in of the kingdom of God. To the Yeats of this poem it is a sphinx-like creature with "a gaze blank and pitiless as the sun," a "rough beast" that, when its hour comes round at last (after "twenty centuries of stony sleep were vexed to nightmare by a rocking cradle"), "slouches towards Bethlehem to be born."[1] Although this vision of the absurd has its place in the larger vision of Yeats's all-too-orderly *Vision,* we may fairly bracket this larger context by noting that it is also a response to a unique and all-too-absurd historical period that must be experienced by those of this century as a linear progression into the void rather than as a cyclical extension of the phases of the moon, as Yeats the gnostic saw it.

"The Second Coming" is an encounter with the absurd, but perhaps because it is set in the larger context of a worldview, or *Weltanschauung,* that ultimately denies all absurdity, it is not yet through and beyond the absurd. For this we must wait for Yeats's later poetry in which the architectonic symmetry of *The Vision* and the poems of Yeats's middle years are replaced by the Crazy Jane poems and the far more grotesque visions of old age.

130

Before we look at these poems we might well look back at "Sailing to Byzantium" which represents a first, nonabsurdist response to old age. "That is no country for old men," the first line of the poem tells us. The rest of the first stanza sets up a contrast between the "young in one another's arms" who, "caught in that sensual music," "neglect monuments of unaging intellect." The whole poem is indeed a plea to go from the living reality to the artifact:

> An aged man is but a paltry thing,
> A tattered coat upon a stick, unless
> Soul clap its hands and sing, and louder sing
> For every tatter in its mortal dress,
> Nor is there singing school but studying
> Monuments of its own magnificence. . . .

These monuments are found in the holy city of Byzantium where ancient mosaic workers build these timeless artifacts. Therefore, the poet prays to the "sages standing in God's holy fire / As in the gold mosaic of a wall" that they be the singing masters of his soul and, liberating him from his sad heart "sick with desire and fastened to a dying animal," "gather me into the artifice of eternity." "Once out of nature," the poet tells us in the last stanza, he shall not take his bodily form from any natural thing but from some artificial nightingale hammered by a Grecian goldsmith to keep a drowsy emperor awake.

There could be no more thorough rejection of the natural passions and instincts in favor of "unaging intellect" than this. A transition from *The Vision* poems to the last poems of Yeats's life is Part IV of "Vacillations," for it is a genuine mystical moment from ordinary life rather than sensual passion, on the one side, or gnostic artifact on the other:

My fiftieth year had come and gone,
I sat, a solitary man,
In a crowded London shop,
An open book and empty cup
On the marble table-top. //
While on the shop and street I gazed
My body of a sudden blazed;
And twenty minutes more or less
It seemed, so great my happiness,
That I was blessèd and could bless.[3]

Actually, this small poem forms a perfect transition to the first of the "Last Poems" that we turn to—"Lapis Lazuli" in which, in contrast to Shakespeare's tragic plays, we are told that Hamlet and Lear are joyous, and, to reinforce this, we are also told of the Chinamen carved in lapis lazuli who gaze on the tragic scene in mountain and sky and play mournful melodies, that, mid many wrinkles, "their ancient, glittering eyes, are gay."[4] This somber joy peering at us through tragedy is a step toward going through and beyond the absurd to holding the tension between affirming and withstanding.

First, however, we must pass through the accentuation of the absurd itself in the Crazy Jane poems, particularly "Crazy Jane Talks with the Bishop." The bishop offers Crazy Jane a heavenly mansion in place of the "foul sty" which is what old age has left for her. Crazy Jane responds that fair and foul are near of kin and fair needs foul. She reminds the bishop that while a woman can be proud and stiff when intent on love, Love itself "has pitched his mansion in the place of excrement." The conclusion represents another step toward holding the tension between affirming and withstanding; for it shows that we must go through the encounter with the absurd to reach the new place where meaning is to be found: "For nothing can be sole or whole / That has not been rent."

The late poem of Yeats's that has always moved me the most is "The Circus Animals' Desertion," written in 1939, the year of his death. Here the poet looks back on the figures he has created through a lifetime of poetry and playwriting and comes through with a humility that has nothing to do with "unaging intellect" or the escape from earthly woe into a sphere of immortal artifacts. "Maybe at last, being but a broken man, I must be satisfied with my heart," the poet laments, "although winter and summer till old age began my circus animals were all on show." After enumerating the figures from his poetry and plays and himself, with his "embittered heart," "starved for the bosom of [his own creation Oisin's] fairy bride," he confesses that "Players and painted stage took all my love, / And not those things that they were emblems of." "Those masterful images because complete / Grew in pure mind." But what did they grow out of? And now the great romantic, who has been called the finest English poet of the twentieth century, acknowledges for his sources refuse, street sweepings, kettles, bottles, broken cans, old iron and bones, even "that raving slut who keeps the till." The conclusion of this master of persona and artifact is one that to me suggests the true beginning of finding meaning through and beyond the absurd:

> Now that my ladder's gone
> I must lie down where all the ladders start,
> In the foul rag-and-bone shop of the heart.[5]

W. H. Auden

"O all the instruments agree / The day of his death was a dark cold day," wrote W. H. Auden (1907-1973) in "In Memory of W. B. Yeats," who died in January 1939. "Earth receive an honoured guest; / William Yeats is laid to rest." But in prophecy of the war that every discerning person knew was soon to come, Auden also wrote in this poem:

> In the nightmare of the dark
> All the dogs of Europe bark,
> And the living nations wait,
> Each sequestered in its hate.

yet he ended on as much of a positive note as he could summon:

> In the deserts of the heart
> Let the healing fountain start,
> In the prison of his days
> Teach the free man how to praise.[6]

Auden was much more explicitly a poet of the absurd than Yeats, as in "Christmas 1940":

> "Beware! Beware! The Great Boyg has you down,"
> Some deeper instinct in revulsion cries,
> "The Void desires to have you for its creature,
> A doll through whom It may ventriloquise
> Its vast resentment as your very own. . . ."[7]

Auden was also, more clearly than Yeats, a religious poet: "Sir, no man's enemy, forgiving all but sin its negative inversion," begins one of his poems. And he was also a compassionate man, not using the aesthetic as a buffer between him and the suffering of his fellowman. "Doom is dark and deeper than any sea dingle / On what man soever it falls," he wrote during the Second World War of the man who was taken from the comforts of home—"kissing his wife between single sheets"—to the far flung corners of the war-torn world. "No cloud-soft hand can hold him, restraint by women."[8]

We can see holding the tension between affirming and withstanding most clearly in Auden's "September 1, 1939," written at the very outbreak of the Second World War. It is from this poem, in fact, that the title of this book is taken. In it he pictures himself sitting in a dive on Fifty-Second Street in New York City, "Uncertain and afraid / As the clever hopes expire / Of a low dishonest decade." Being an intellectual he can summon Luther and Thucydides to explain the psychopathic god [Hitler] and "what dictators do / The elderly rubbish they talk / To an apathetic grave." The skyscrapers of New York City proclaim "the strength of Collective Man" but cannot obscure the international wrong or make us lose sight of "Children afraid of the night / Who have never been happy or good" and are "Lost in a haunted wood."

For all the patent absurdity of this situation, an absurdity now fully manifest and world-wide, Auden ends, not merely on a positive note, but with a clear evocation of the meaning found in affirming in the face of negation and despair:

> Defenceless under the night
> Our world in stupor lies;
> Yet, dotted everywhere,
> Ironic points of light
> Flash out wherever the Just

Exchange their messages:
May I, composed like them
Of Eros and of dust,
Beleaguered by the same
Negation and despair,
Show an affirming flame.[9]

Pablo Neruda

In contrast to Denise Levertov who combines social concern and religious attitude in equal measure, Pablo Neruda comes down almost entirely on the side of social concern, mixed with marvelous distillations from his personal life. "Gautama Christ," one of Neruda's rare poems that is explicitly religious, deliberately juxtaposes names from two quite separate religions both as a deconstruction of religious sentiment and as a way of pointing to his subject: the names of God. Actually Neruda says nothing about the Buddha but only about God's "representative . . . called Jesus or Christ," a name "which has been used up, worn down and deposited on the riverbank of our lives like empty mollusk shells." But this poem is not satire, like T. S. Eliot's famous satire on the church, "The Hippopotamus." He recognizes that something endures: "an agate lip, an iridescent footprint still shimmering in the light."

The second stanza begins with the names of God being spoken by the best and the worst, the clean and the dirty, but it spells out only the worst: "blood-stained assassins / and golden brown victims who blazed with napalm, / while Nixon with the hands / of Cain blessed those he had condemned to death . . ." The third and

136

final stanza preserves those values that the poet feels there is to preserve in these names of God: "Because they reminded us / of our ancestors, of the first humans, of those who asked questions, / of those who found the hymn that united them in mystery."[10]

Neruda touches on our theme of going through and beyond the absurd in *Extravagaria* as in his poem "With Her" in which, recognizing that the time is difficult, the poet asks his beloved to wait for him so that together they can live it out vividly, rise and suffer, feel and rejoice, letting "our difficult time / stand up to infinity."[11]

In "The Poet's Obligation," the first poem of Neruda's *Fully Empowered*, Neruda sees his destiny as keeping the sea's lamenting in his consciousness so that wherever people are imprisoned, he may be present to them in an errant wave. "So, through me, freedom and the sea will call in answer to the shrouded heart." In "Investigations" the poet reflects that when he gave up shaking the earth, he thought others would bestow on him a little thanks or a smile but found instead that they pointed a finger at his life and scrutinized him with an indignant eye. Despite "such corruption" he does not demand two eyes for an eye or a hand for a fingernail. "I made an unbreakable pledge to myself / that the people would find their voices in my song." In the title poem, "Fully Empowered," the poet sees himself as poised between life and death, being and non-being: "what there is of death surrounding me / opens in me a window out to living."[12]

Neruda's most impressive contribution to going through and beyond the absurd to affirmation and withstanding is his elegy, "To the Dead Poor Man." The "poor man" who is being buried today was always so badly off that this is the first time that his person is personified. He did not have house, land, good food, or any of the other things that make life tolerable. Yet from bishop to judge everybody assured him of his share of heaven, and now he will have so much sky that he will not know what to do with it. He who plowed the land cruelly on earth can plow it easily in heaven where he brings as his fortune sixty years of hunger. Never having hoped for much justice, his cup is suddenly so filled that "he has fallen dumb with happiness." By his weight alone those who lift him on their shoulders know how many things he always lacked. If he did not have shoes or "justice in life, and all men beat him and . . . did him down," and even so he went on laboring away, "now at least we know how much he didn't have, / that we did not help him in his life on the earth."[13] This is not just a social satire on the part of the communist Neruda at the expense of the false consolations of religion. It is also a deeply concrete, concerned, and compassionate statement that cannot fail to move us. It confronts evil and the absurd and finds meaning on the far side of them.

Czeslaw Milosz

Czeslaw Milosz is a Lithuanian-Polish poet, essayist, and novelist who encountered so much of the absurd under the Nazi and Communist occupations of his country that his very act of writing meaningful poetry is in itself a movement through and beyond the absurd to the tension between affirming and withstanding. In the postwar period he moved to America, became a professor at the University of California in Berkeley, and received the Nobel Prize for Literature. His little poem "How It Was" from *Bells in Winter* lingers in the absurd rather than moves through and beyond it. Wandering deep into the mountains he saw "the mighty power of counter-fulfillment," "the penalty of a promise lost forever." No one implored, everyone whispered in loneliness, "I cannot live any longer." None of the bearded messengers who founded clandestine communes in the cities announced the birth of a child-savior. Expeditionary soldiers took part in forbidden rites, not looking for any hope. "And those who longed for the Kingdom took refuge like me in the / mountains to become the last heirs of a dishonored myth."[14]

Milosz is clearly a religious man but one who has to recover his religion again and again in the teeth of the negative and of denial. A patient pilgrim who notched the months and years on his stick, he found his way to the upper chapel to behold a wooden Madonna surrounded by a throng of impassive art lovers. Crossing mountains and valleys through flames, wide water, and unfaithful memory, he encounters "The same passion but I hear no call. / And the holy had its abode only in denial."[15]

It is in Milosz's most recent book of poetry, *Provinces*, that Milosz moves to an affirmation in the midst of his encounter with the absurd. "I had to find a core that makes all things real," he wrote in "A New Province," "Always hoping to reach it the next day."

The poem "Inheritor" begins with a contrast between the events those of the poet's generation know and the youth who do not know them: "You do not seek / Faith and hope as they were practiced here." Yet the poet says, "the same ecstasy of discovering things unite us":

> You will find again
> The sacredness they tried to expel forever.
> Something returns, invisible, frail and shy,
> Adoring, without name, and yet fearless.[16]

In "Meditation" the poet suggests that people were mistaken in praising God as a ruler on a throne who protects them. He sees God rather as one who wanted to help people, felt compassion for them, and forgave them their mistakes, falsity, and ugliness. The poet has learned at least what it means to love people and why love is worn down by loneliness, pity, and anger. The end of the poem is a prayer, a supplication to God "to perceive the greatness of those—weak—creatures / Who are able to be honest, brave in misfortune, and patient till / the end."[17]

The absurd is certainly real for Milosz, but the movement through and beyond the absurd is still more real, and it enables him to affirm even in the face of his own approaching death: He rejoices that the "large finger-like leaves of an Hawaiian fern . . . will be when I am no more."[18]

In "Meaning" he goes beyond this joy to an affirmation which is at once trusting and contending, a movement through and beyond the absurd which needs no overarching worldview. "When I die, I will see the lining of the world. . . . The true meaning, ready to be decoded." But if he does not find such a meaning, there will still be a tireless messenger who "calls out, protests, screams."[19]

9

The Scandal of the Particular

Yehuda Amichai

The title of this chapter unites the celebration of the particular with the encounter with evil and the absurd which leads us through and beyond the absurd to affirmation in the midst of withstanding.

Yehuda Amichai was born in Germany in 1924 to an orthodox Jewish family that emigrated to Palestine in 1936. Although his poetry has always been written in Hebrew from 1948 on, he was influenced in particular by Auden and, to a lesser extent, Eliot. His loving relationship to his religious father and his ambivalent relationship to the God of his fathers, in addition to his life experience of moving from one war to another, have made him a perfect channel for the Dialogue with the Absurd. Amichai would fain be rid of the God of his fathers:

In another continent of time,
the dread rabbis of my childhood appear,
holding the gravestones high over
their heads.
Bound up with the knot of my life.
My God, my God,
Why have you not forsaken me!?[1]

In another poem the question is reversed and becomes a cry of
anguish of the "collector of pain in the tradition of this country":

My God, my God, why? Have you forsaken me?
My God, my God. Even then you had to call him twice.
The second time already a question, a first doubt: my God?[2]

When Amichai was a child, his parents stitched his handker-
chief to the corner of his pocket so he would not commit the sin of
carrying something on the Holy Sabbath. Since then God's
"thunder has rolled back and become a great silence." His eyes
"have opened wider and wider from year to year . . . to the rim of
pain" and to death, which is "not sleep but open eyes, the whole
body gaping with eyes, pressed in the narrow space of the world."[3]

"God has pity on kindergarten children," Amichai wrote in
1955.

He has less pity on school children.
And on grownups he has no pity at all,
he leaves them alone,
and sometimes they must crawl on all fours
in the burning sand
to reach the first-aid station
covered with blood.[4]

142

And in "Ibn Gabirol," at this same time, he wrote: "Through the wound in my chest / God peers into the universe." Amichai has measured his life in wars, and war is one of his most frequent absurdist themes:

> And because of the war I say again,
> For the sake of a last and simple sweetness:
> The sun is circling round the earth Yes.
> The earth is flat, like a lost, floating board Yes.
> God is in Heaven Yes . . .
> They've made me a commander of the dead
> on the Mount of Olives.
> Always, even in victory,
> I lose.[5]

   T. S. Eliot shocked the poetic world in "Prufrock" by comparing the evening stretched out against the sky to a patient etherized upon a table. Amichai is still more shocking, even for us latecomers whom very little shocks: "God's hand is in the world like my mother's hand in the guts of a slaughtered chicken on Sabbath eve."[6] In a similar but even stronger and more paradoxical image, Amichai follows the statement

> "How beautiful are thy tents, Jacob."
> Even now, when there are neither tents nor Jacob's
> tribes, I say, how beautiful,

with:

> Then my mouth will open wide
> in everlasting praise,
> open like the belly of a

143

wide-open calf hung on a hook
in a butcher's shop of the Old City market.[7]

"Into God's closed book we shall be put," Amichai wrote in "My Mother and Me," "and there we shall rest to mark for him the page where he stopped reading." "God is angry with me," he wrote in 1967, "because I always force him to create the world once again from chaos, light, second day, until man, and back to the beginning."[8] This burgeons in his 1976 "Songs of Zion the Beautiful" into a full-fledged absurdist vision of God's relation with the world:

> Every evening God takes his glittery merchandise
> out of the shop window:
> chariot works, tables of law, fancy beads,
> crosses and gleaming bells,
> and puts them back into dark boxes
> inside, and closes the shutter: "Another day
> and still not one prophet has come to buy."[9]

"Someone told me he's going down to Sinai because he wants to be alone with his God," Amichai wrote in "Relativity," and concludes this statement and the poem with: "I warned him." "God will bring the dead back to life, maybe," Amichai wrote in "A Song About a Photograph,"

> But he won't put torn things together
> Nor will he close the cracks.
> Even the one in the street in front of your home
> Will get longer and widen into the world.[10]

In "A Song of Lies on Sabbath Eve," the poet pictures himself as lying to his father, saying he went to another synagogue when he went to none at all. Then he pictures the sabbath itself as a lie:

> And in all the houses at night
> hymns and lies drifted up together,
> *O taste and see,*
> and in all the houses at night
> Sabbath angels died like flies in the lamp,
> and lovers put mouth to mouth
> and inflated one another till they floated in the air
> or burst

Since then lying has tasted very sweet to the poet, and when his father died he returned his son's lie about going to another synagogue by saying that he was going to another life.[11]

In "The Diameter of the Bomb" from 1978, Amichai gives us a vision of the Absurd without God: an ever-enlarging circle of those killed and maimed by the bomb until the entire world is included in its circumference.

> And I won't even mention the crying of orphans
> That reaches up to the throne of God and
> beyond, making
> a circle with no end and no God.[12]

Yet even here there are positive notes as when the poet sees an Arab shepherd searching for his goat on Mount Zion while he is looking for his little boy. After both the goat and the boy are found among the bushes "and our voices came back inside us, laughing and crying," the poet announces: "Searching for a goat or a son / has always been the beginning / of a new religion in these mountains."[13] The most positive statement of all[14] is found in the first stanza of his 1978 poem "Near the Wall of a House":

> Near the wall of a house painted
> to look like stone,
> I saw visions of God.
> A sleepless night that gives others a headache
> gave me flowers
> opening beautifully inside my brain.
> And he who was lost like a dog
> will be found like a human being
> and brought back home again.[15]

"Quiet Joy" gives us a mixed message of a joy found too late, after having done great injustice to oneself and to others but nonetheless, "A few months more for quiet joy."[16] And "Letter of Recommendation" suggests at least a temporary reconciliation with his father and his father's God:

> During the day I walk about,
> The Ten Commandments on my lips
> like an old song someone is humming to himself. . . .
> I remember my father waking me up
> for early prayers. He did it caressing
> my forehead, not tearing the blanket away.
> Since then I love him even more.
> And because of this
> let him be woken up
> gently and with love
> on the Day of Resurrection.[17]

The poet's reconciliation with his father and God does not mean that Amichai shares the orthodox Jewish belief in the resurrection of the dead. "I'm on my way from believing in God and you're on your way toward it," he wrote in a poem about his son.[18] From his own Dialogue with the Absurd, the poet has pasted together for himself a new Bible with which he now lives "censored and pasted and limited and in peace":

> I've filtered out of the Book of Esther the residue
> of vulgar joy, and out of the Book of Jeremiah
> the howl of pain in the guts. And out of the
> Song of Songs the endless search for love,
> and out of the Book of Genesis the dreams
> and Cain, and out of Ecclesiastes
> the despair and out of the Book of Job—Job.[19]

What Amichai means by filtering "out of the Book of Job—Job" is suggested by his savage poem on Job:

> I want to make a bet with Job
> on how God and Satan will behave:
> who will be the first to curse man.
> Like sunset red in Job's mouth
> He was beaten and his last word
> sinks, red, into his last face. . . .
> "To hell with it, Job. Cursed be the day
> You were created in my image. You are
> Your mother's shame, Job."
> God cursed, God blessed. Job won.
> And I must kill myself with the toy
> pistol of my small son.[20]

"I am a man 'planted beside streams of water,'" Amichai wrote in an allusion to Psalm 1, "but I'm not 'blessed be the man.'" "My father is dead, and God is only one, like me." All he can do with all this water is weep it, sweat it, and urinate it and slip it from his wounds. At the cemetery of Messilat Zion in the mountains of Jerusalem, the poet sees the Luf flower growing half hidden, and it reminds him "of deep and terrible things in my life." "Does salvation grow out of all this?" he asks himself "And what are its seeds?"[21] Yet none of this is negation. Amichai, too, like the English poet W. H. Auden, shows an affirming flame.[22] He does so in terms of the present and the everyday rather than some heaven or apocalyptic future. When he banged his head on the door or when he stroked the hand of his beloved, Amichai did not scream or whisper "mother" or "God" nor did he "speak of the vision of the End of Days / of a world where there will be no heads and doors anymore" or "of hands stroking heads in the wide-opening heavens." He simply said, like the Zen Buddhist, "My head Door Your hand."[23]

In the end Amichai's moving through and beyond the absurd to affirmation in the midst of contending includes God, although it is a sad God—sad in himself and sad about the world:

I saw
the Lord of the world in all his sadness,
a radar God, lonely, circling round and round
with his huge wings, with sad movements
of primordial doubt.
Yes yes and no no, with the sadness of a God who knows
that there is no reply and no decision: only turning.
What he sees makes him sad. And what
he doesn't see makes him sad. What he records
is the code of sadness for humans to decipher.[24]

Like Elie Wiesel, who speaks of how God and man exchanged places and how the duel between them continues with infinite remorse and infinite yearning, Amichai sees God and man as involved in a mutual mistake:

> Everyone hears a step at night,
> not only prisoners, everyone hears.
> Everything is steps at night,
> receding or approaching,
> but never arriving close enough
> to be touched. That is man's
> mistake about God and God's mistake about man[25]

Denise Levertov

Although Denise Levertov is clearly a believing and devout Christian, there is much in her poetry that comes close to the attitude that we have described as the Dialogue with the Absurd. Nor does she see this attitude as an exclusively modern one, as suggested by "The Showings," her meditations on that remarkable medieval English mystic Lady Julian of Norwich (1342–1416) whom T. S. Eliot quotes at the end of *Four Quartets*. Although Lady Julian laughed aloud, "glad with a *most high inward happiness*," she recognized that there are deeds done so evil and injuries inflicted so great that it seems impossible that any good might come of them or any redemption transform them.

> She lived in dark times, as we do:
> war, and the Black Death, hunger, strife,

torture, massacre She knew
all of this, she felt it
sorrowfully, mournfully,
shaken as men shake
a cloth in the wind.

But the poet turns to Lady Julian, who clung to joy through tears
and sweat and blood and, like an acrobat on a high wire, fiercely
held on by her teeth to her certainty of infinite mercy, witnessed
with outward and inward sight: *"Love was his meaning."*[26]

Reflecting on Rilke's *Book of Hours*, Levertov recognizes that
if all motion and the swing of cause and effect, attention and
thought, could come to a halt, then she, too, like the mystic Rilke
pictures, could fill with God "to the very brim, / bounding the
whole flood of your boundlessness: / and at that timeless moment
of possession" surrender God and let God flow back into all creation. But she recognizes as well not just for herself but for all of
us, that there will never be that stillness within the pulse of flesh
and the dust of being where we trudge: "What we desire travels
with us. / We must breathe time as fishes breathe water. / God's
flight circles us."[27] Nonetheless, in "Intimation" she grows impa-
tient with the blue of the sky and the rhythm of days, knowing that
a different need has begun to cast its lines out from her into a place
unknown. "I reach for a silence almost present, elusive among my
heartbeats."[28]

At the same time, Levertov continues to reach outward, as in
her long libretto for the oratorio "El Salvador: Requiem and Invocation," and here she touches again on the Dialogue with the
Absurd. The names and bodies of all those martyred for the cause
of humanity tell us that horror won't cease on the earth until the
hungry are fed, that the fruits of the earth don't grow that a few may
profit.

that injustice here
is one with injustice anywhere,
all of us *are*
our brother's keepers,
members one of another
responsible, culpable, and—
able to change.
This is the knowledge
that grows in power
out of the seeds of their martyrdom.[29]

In "The Love of Morning" the Dialogue with the Absurd moves from specific social injustice to human evil in general: "we've lain in the dark crying out / O God, save us from the horror." Despite all this, "God has saved the world one more day / even with its leaden burden of human evil." We wake to birdsong, and our hearts are lifted, "swung like laughing infants." If we keep on because of "our own hunger, the dear tasks of continuance, the footsteps before us in the earth's belovèd dust, leading the way," it is still hard to love again. "We resent a summons that disregards our sloth, and this calls us, calls us."[30]

In "The Task" Levertov offers a long meditation on a God who somehow manages to turn our suffering into meaning. In the first stanza God is pictured as an old man sitting about upstairs in sleeveless undershirt or asleep with arms folded and stomach rumbling, the breath from his open mouth strident, presaging death. This picture is rejected in the second stanza for one of God as in the wilderness next door in the huge tundra room with no walls and a sky roof, busy at the loom. Absorbed in his continuous work God hears the humming of bees but only far-off our screams. "Our voices . . . can't stop their terrible beseeching."[31]

151

Elsewhere I say regarding the little priest in Bernanos's novel *The Diary of a Country Priest* that his suffering and confusion cannot be seen entirely within the classical mystical pattern of St. John of the Cross' "dark night of the soul" but must also be understood as part of the problematic of the divided modern person.[32] This is also stated in her way by Levertov in "Oblique Prayer":

> Not the profound *dark*
> *night of the soul //*
> and not the austere desert
> to scorch the heart at noon,
> grip the mind
> in teeth of ice at evening //
> but gray,
> a place
> without clear outlines, //
> the air
> heavy and thick //
> the soft ground clogging
> my feet if I walk,
> sucking them downwards
> if I stand. / . . .
> [It is] a part of human-ness //
> to enter
> no man's land? //
> I can remember . . .
> the blessèd light that caressed the world
> before I stumbled into
> this place of mere
> darkness [33]

Annie Dillard

If Annie Dillard's "quirky facts" and "scandal of the particular" make her an exemplar of the mysticism of the particular, as we have seen, they also bring her into the Dialogue with the Absurd. Dillard contemplates the mystery of "the created universe, spanning an unthinkable void with an unthinkable profusion of forms" and of "nothingness, those sickening reaches of time in either direction." "Have we rowed out to the thick darkness," she asks, "or are we all playing pinochle in the bottom of the boat?" "After thousands of years we're still strangers to darkness, fearful aliens in an enemy camp with our arms crossed over our chests." She contemplates the mystery of cruelty and the waste of pain, but she also wonders about "another mystery: the inrush of power and light, the canary that sings on the skull . . . beauty, a grace wholly gratuitous."[34] She writes a whole essay on "Intricacy": "Even on the perfectly ordinary and clearly visible level, creation carries on with an intricacy unfathomable and apparently uncalled for. . . . You open the door and all heaven and hell break loose." What is true of the visible is still more true of what is not visible: "Mystery itself is as fringed and intricate as the shape of the air in time." Nature exults in radicality, extremism, anarchy: "If we were to judge nature by its common sense or likelihood, we wouldn't believe the world existed." But her wonder does not stop here. It ranges from the monstrous to the beautiful:

> The wonder is—given the errant nature of freedom and the burgeoning of texture in time—the wonder is that all the forms are not monsters, that there is beauty at all, grace gratuitous, pennies found, like mockingbird's free fall. Beauty itself is the fruit of the creator's exuberance that grew such a tangle, and the

grotesques and horrors bloom from that same free growth, that intricate scramble and twine up and down the conditions of time.[35]

Dillard can contemplate the love of God for each particular and suggest that it is our lack of imagination that makes it so hard to believe in that. Yet in her extraordinary book *Holy the Firm*, prompted in part by the terrible fate of her friend Julie, burned beyond recognition in an airplane fire, Dillard brings into full focus the absurd itself and our encounter with it, prior to the dialogue that finds meaning in that encounter. God "has abandoned us," she writes, "slashing creation loose at its base from any roots in the real." Julie, evidence of things seen (a play on St. Paul's definition of faith), causes her to look at "world stuff" appalled and declare that God "treats us less well than we treat our lawns. . . . Of faith I have nothing, only of truth: that this one God is a brute and traitor, abandoning us to time, to necessity and the engines of matter unhinged." If God has no hand in all this, if God has no hand but is a holy fire burning self-contained for power's sake alone and the rest of us go hang, "Then the accidental universe spins mute, obedient only to its own gross terms, meaningless, out of mind, and alone."[36]

> If days are gods, then gods are dead, and artists pyrotechnic fools. Time is a hurdy-gurdy, a lampoon, and death's a bawd. We're beheaded by the nick of time. We're logrolling on a falling world, on time released from meaning and rolling loose, . . . a bauble flung and forgotten, lapsed, and the gods on the lam.[37]

Dillard's plaint and complaint extends from God to ourselves. "God burgeons up or showers down into the shabbiest of occasions, and leaves his creation's dealings with him in the hands of

154

purblind and clumsy amateurs." "Who shall stand on God's holy hill?" Dillard questions with Psalm 24, but replaces the clean hand and pure heart which the Psalm answers with "us"—a generation unfit and unready, "having each of us chosen wrongly, made a false start, failed, yielded to impulse and the tangled comfort of pleasures, and grown exhausted, unable to seek the thread, weak, and involved."[38]

We need reminding that God cannot or will not "catch time in its free fall and stick a nickel's worth of sense into our days," and that time, in its turn, must only churn out enormity at random, that we are created sojourners in a land we did not make, with no meaning of itself and no meaning we can make for it alone. The world is patently unredeemed, Dilliard suggests at one point, the entire rest of the universe irrelevant and nonparticipant—"time and matter unreal and so unknowable, an illusory, absurd, accidental, and overelaborate stage."[39]

Taking off from what Buber says about the crisis of the primitive world in its movement from the sacred to the profane, Dillard suggests that the whole world now seems not-holy: "We have drained the light from the boughs in the sacred grove and snuffed it in the high places and along the banks of sacred streams." As a result, speech has perished from among lifeless things, "and living things say very little to very few." We try in vain to call God back to the mountain and pray till we're blue in the face. We give our whole lives to listening, and nothing happens. Silence has become not our heritage but our destiny. Silence is not suppression, it is all there is. We are here to witness and watch the whole inhuman array, knowing our meaningful activity scarcely covers the terrain of the earth.[40]

Alternating between thinking of our planet as a dear and familiar home and as a land of exile in which we are all sojourners, Dilliard comes down on the side of the latter, especially in times of sorrow. We find ourselves set among the other creatures "as among lifelike props for a tragedy—or a broad lampoon—on a thrust rock stage."

> The planet itself is a sojourner in airless space, a wet ball flung across nowhere. The few objects in the universe scatter. The coherence of matter dwindles and crumbles toward stillness.[41]

Nonetheless, as we have seen, Dillard ends not just by *encountering* the evil and the absurd but by going through and beyond it to the place where she can affirm in the midst of withstanding, and she does so, not just with stillness and silence but a meaningful voice that arises from our meeting it and listening to the silence:

> The silence is all there is. It is the alpha and the omega. It is God's brooding over the face of the waters; it is the blended note of the ten thousand things, the whine of wings. You take a step in the right direction to pray to this silence, and even to address the prayer to "World." Distinctions blur. Quit your tents. Pray without ceasing.[42]

10

The Shoah—
Our Ultimate Confrontation

André Schwarz-Bart, *The Last of the Just*

Our discussion of the encounter with evil and the Dialogue with the Absurd leads us inexorably to confront the challenge of the *Shoah*—that historical event which is paradigmatic of the absurdity of our time and of all human history.

According to the Talmud, the world stands because of the *zaddik*—the "just man," the righteous person who is justified by God. In Jewish tradition this expanded into the legend of the *lamedvovnikim*—the thirty-six anonymous zaddikim who exist in every generation and because of whom the world is not destroyed. In his epic novel *The Last of the Just* the one-time Polish Jew and French writer André Schwarz-Bart conflates this legend with that of the *kiddush ha-Shem*—that sanctification of the name of God which is accomplished by Jewish martyrs from Rabbi Akiba on

157

down. *The Last of the Just* begins in the twelfth century in England and follows the fortunes of one single family—the Levys—who since the martyrdom of Yom Tov Levy in York have never been without a "just man."

At first the novel reads like a historical chronicle. Then, in the most recent times recounted, it gives us detailed pictures of the lives of Mordecai and Judith Levy, of their son Benjamin and his family, and, most of all, of their grandson Ernie Levy, who is raised in the tradition of the just man and holds it as ideal and model. Ernie never really believes he himself is one, and yet, in the end, he is certainly not only a just man of the Levys but an anonymous just man whom God has chosen—for unbelievable suffering and special neglect.

The encounter with the Absurd is already hinted at in the irony with which each story of martyrdom is told and continues in ever growing momentum until it cascades to heights that are scarcely believable. Yet in the gentleness, tenderness, and warmth of Ernie Levy and the loving detail with which his life is described we can discern, unmistakably, the Dialogue with the Absurd.

Some of the account is almost whimsical, such as the time when Ernie leaves home because no one understands him and for one night becomes "the just man of the flies." Later, after Herr Kremer—the only teacher who defends the Jewish pupils— has been removed and Ilse—the only student who has been Ernie's friend—has succumbed to the general pressure and applauded when the other students beat Ernie and spit on him and pull his pants down, Ernie tries unsuccessfully to kill himself. Though after two years in the hospital he recovers up to a point, both his patriarchal grandfather, Mordecai, and he himself recognize that "death had set its hand upon his spirit." After his grandmother Judith visits him in the hospital where he lies imprisoned in straps, buckles, tubes, and a mask, leaving room for one eye and his mouth, Ernie's past invades him "like a river in flood":

158

with torn tree trunks here and there, babies' cradles floating, animals belly-up, figures on the roofs, Ilse on a boat manned by grimacing creatures and the Levys' poor Noah's ark wandering among the flotsam, all of them raising their arms to God, who looked down inscrutably. The world was going to rack and ruin, though no one seemed to notice . . . No one noticed that the river was flowing beneath the beds, carrying off the whole hospital in its slow, cruel course.[1]

Ernie trains himself in boxing and occasionally beats some of the Hitler youth who attack him and his little brother. Yet he cannot bring his spirit to hate them or to hate Ilse. That worries him greatly and fills him with shame. "He considered himself a traitor to the cause of the Levys." On November 6, 1938, a Jewish adolescent named Herschel Grynzpan shot a Nazi diplomat in Paris after his parents had been deported to a concentration camp. Awaiting the oncoming Nazi storm, the Levys consulted among themselves as to what to do. At that time Mordecai still believed that the Nazis would take everything but not their lives. "The Germans aren't altogether savages, they aren't Ukrainians." But even he cannot understand what is happening to them and his son Benjamin still less. "My dear children," says the pious Mordecai, "there are days when I myself do not understand the will of God too well."

"For a thousand years all over Europe, how many of our women and children have been martyred—not with the peaceful awareness of the Just Men but with the terrified little souls of lambs? And what good," the old man went on in great grief, "is suffering that does not serve to glorify the Name? Why all the *useless* persecutions? . . . But after all, are we Jews not the sacrificial tribute, the tribute of suffering that man—uh—offers to God?" . . .

"Ah, my dear father!" Benjamin said then, brokenhearted,

"if all that were God's will, who would not rejoice? But I think we are the prey of the wicked—simply a prey."[2]

During the *Kristallnacht,* or Night of the Broken Glass, on November 10, 1938, the Nazis avenged a hundredthousandfold the murder. Faced with the fact that there were no limits to the Nazi persecution of the Jews, the Levy family barricaded themselves in the attic, ready to defend their sacred books with their lives, and after the pogrom was over took all the worldly goods that they could carry and crossed over the bridge at Kehl to France. The Western democracies responded to the Nazi terror by refusing visas to the Jews and sinking or turning back the ships full of Jewish women and children who sought refuge outside of Germany.

In France Ernie enlists in the army, thereby obtaining eight certificates that he hopes will protect the other members of the Levy family from being deported. He remembers a legend that Mordecai told of a tiny hunchback who asked a rabbi how he could have been born that way if God created a perfect world. "But little animal, sweet little soul," the rabbi quickly replied with a delicate hint of reproach, *"for a hunchback you're as perfect as can be. . . . Right?"* Ernie is repelled by this bittersweet philosophy:

> That the world bore a fantastic, enormous hump of suffering was not a matter for joking. For his part, he knew that the Most High—blessed be his name throughout the centuries—had endowed him notably with a matrix made to measure, crystalline and cold and transparent as glass, imprisoning him body and soul, and reflecting with tearless perfection the white ward in the hospital, the gleaming light of the pogrom, the delicately blue sky of suburban Paris, and this dawn, stinking delicately of blood and gnawed at by a swarm of Junkers.[3]

160

Even imprisoned in this protective matrix, Ernie feels that the fall of France and the complete delivery of his family to Nazi extermination camps is the straw that breaks the camel's back. He thinks for the second time of hanging himself and never forgives himself for not going through with it. Instead Ernie sets out deliberately to turn himself into a dog and spends a number of years barking and eating raw meat, half cynical and half mad. After this he goes to a farm in the Rhone valley and lives with the woman who is running it in the absence of her husband until a man recognizes him as a Jew through the depth and intensity of his eyes.

Leaving the comparative safety of unoccupied France, Ernie goes to Paris where he meets the last contingent of old men who come from his home of Zemyock and who pay him great honor as one of the Levys. When they discover that he is not thirty years old, as he appears, but the twenty-year-old grandson of Mordecai, they recall how his grandfather spoke of him as "certain to be called to the destiny of a Just Man. 'Not a Just Man of the Levys,' he said, 'but a true Unknown Just, an Inconsolable—one of those whom God dares not even caress with his little finger.'"[4] Ernie lives with these four old men, but he does not share their piety:

> Ernie was amazed that the men of Marais never tired of God. In a tiny block of houses condemned to disappear shortly in the great flood of death, they went on waving their arms to heaven, clinging to it in all their fervor, in all their torment, in all their pious despair. Each day the Nazi raids netted relatives or friends . . . but the little synagogues . . . were never empty.[5]

Occasionally Ernie thought of joining one of the resistance movements, but he knew that no matter how many Germans he killed it would not pay for one innocent head, and he had no intention of glorifying himself through a luxurious death, "of separating himself from the humble procession of the Jewish people."

One day Ernie rescues a crippled girl named Golda who is being attacked by four men and, to her amazement, refuses to part from her. He tells her that Jesus was really a good Jew, like the Baal Shem Tov—

> a merciful man and gentle. The Christians say they love him, but I think they hate him without knowing it. So they take the cross by the other end and make a sword out of it and strike us with it![6]

When Golda weeps because she knows they are condemned, Ernie finds those tears more bitter than death and complains to God how the oppressed are naked to the violence of their oppressors and there is no one to console them. Golda asks Ernie to "marry" her because tomorrow it may be too late. Indeed, the day after they make love Golda and her family are taken to the internment center at Drancy. Ernie forces his way in there, arousing the suspicion of the Nazis who torture him "down all the steps that lead to nothingness, making him less than a Jew, less even than an animal, reducing him to a mere object." In his delirium Ernie imagines that Golda and he are being married in a real wedding with all of his family there, and that afterward he hurries to join them in the "little train" which is about to leave. When they tell him enthusiastically that they were waiting for him but thought he wasn't coming, the Ernie of this vision sighs and says,

> Should I be the only Jew left? . . . Every drop of my blood cries out for you. Know that where you are, there am I. If they beat you, am I not in pain? If they gouge out your eyes, am I not blind? And if you take this little train, am I not aboard?[7]

"Can we rise as far as heaven to ask God why things are as they are?" sings the fiddler, and Ernie, recognizing that "separation from a loved one is the most painful foretaste of death. . . . cries out in his dream. Cries out. Cries out. Cries out."

Those in Drancy who had found out about the "final solution" kept silent. Even if they had spoken it aloud, "none would have believed them, for the soul is the slave of life." In the infirmary they call Ernie *Gribouille*, i.e., simpleton. The doctor with a medal of the virgin around his neck and the yellow star of a Jew on his jacket, confesses to the *Gribouille* that when he found out he was one-eighth Jewish at first he was ashamed and felt that he had crucified Our Lord. Later he became terribly shamed of the part of him that was not Jewish and thought of how two thousand years of Christology had prepared the way for the Holocaust. He loved the person of the Christ more than ever, but "not the blond Christ of the cathedrals any more, the glorious Saviour put to death by the Jews." "He's *something else*," he said in the suddenly Jewish, miserable tone of a prisoner and surprised Ernie and the neighboring patients by breaking into sobs.

Ernie found the listless, unhappy Golda in Drancy, begged food and candy for her, and insisted on accompanying her when she was deported to a death camp in Poland. After the interminable ride in the freight car, Ernie went into the gas chamber with Golda and the children, comforting them as best he could, while "with dying arms he embraced Golda's body in an already unconscious gesture of loving protection." But the author, instead of singling Ernie out, tells us "so it was for millions, who turned from *Luftmenschen* into *Luft*" (from individuals living in the spirit to the smoke of the crematoria). Interspersing praise of the Lord with the names of the death camps, the author confesses that while at times one's heart could break in sorrow, he often "can't help thinking that Ernie Levy, dead six million times, is still alive somewhere."

Yesterday, as I stood in the street trembling in despair, rooted to the spot, a drop of pity fell from above upon my face. But there was no breeze in the air, no cloud in the sky. . . . There was only a presence.[8]

Ernie, André Schwarz-Bart's anonymous "Just Man," is not a saint or even, despite the resemblances, a Christ figure. He is Isaiah's "suffering servant" in exactly the terms in which Martin Buber describes him in the last section of his *The Prophetic Faith*: Only in the depths of suffering does the servant discover the mystery of "the God of the sufferers," namely, that "the *zaddik*, the man justified by God, suffers for the sake of God and of His work of salvation, and God is with him in his suffering." Is this not the meaning of the tear of pity that drops on our despairing author out of a cloudless sky and that he can describe only as "a presence"? There is a succession of servants from Abraham, Job, Isaiah, and Jesus to the Yehudi of Buber's Hasidic chronicle-novel *For the Sake of Heaven* and Ernie Levy. In suffering for the sake of God, the servant comes to recognize that God suffers with him and that he is working together with God for the redemption of the world. It is laid on the servant to inaugurate God's new order of peace and justice for the world, a kingdom that now signifies in reality all the human world. Yet there remains a special tie between the personal servant and the servant Israel. Before the third stage of fulfilled messianism, which to Buber, André Schwarz-Bart, and Elie Wiesel alike is clearly unthinkable in an unredeemed world, there is a second stage in which Israel and mankind persistently live—that of the work of suffering. Here the unity between the personal servant and the servant Israel passes over to their unity in suffering. Living and writing in a time just after the greatest suffering that the diaspora had ever known, Buber undoubtedly had the extermination of the Jews by the Nazis in mind when he spoke of this unity

164

of the personal servant and the servant Israel in the willing acceptance of suffering:

> As far as the great suffering of Israel's dispersion was not com-
> pulsory suffering only, but suffering in truth willingly borne, not
> passive but active, it is interpreted in the image of the servant.
> Whosoever accomplishes in Israel the active suffering of Israel,
> he is the servant, and he is Israel, in whom YHVH "glorifies
> Himself." The mystery of history is the mystery of a representa-
> tion which at bottom is identity. The arrow, which is still con-
> cealed in the quiver, is people and man as one.[9]

There is no question that Ernie Levy is a suffering servant in
exactly the sense in which Buber interprets it, namely, one who
takes the great suffering voluntarily on himself—not only his own
personal suffering but that of all Israel and all mankind. Yet we are
left with a mystery which Ernie's grandfather and father have
already enunciated: What is the meaning of the suffering of those
in Israel and those in mankind who do not take it voluntarily on
themselves, but are like that chicken of which Benjamin spoke to
his father who does not rejoice in that it serves to glorify God but
"is altogether sorry—and *reasonably* so—to have been born as a
chicken, slaughtered as a chicken and eaten as a chicken." Perhaps we could enunciate another mystery here: to be a Jew is not
only to be the most exposed person in the modern world, as Buber
pointed out at the beginning of the Nazi regime, but also to be a
person who lives in the tension of not being able to escape from the
fact of being born as a Jew and of accepting and affirming one's
existence as a Jew.

This mystery cannot be dispelled by any theology that justifies
the suffering of the Jew in the name of some divine plan. Once,
many years ago, when I was staying at the home of my friend Emil

Fackenheim in Toronto, a rabbi who was there complained that when asked at a public lecture for a theological justification of the Holocaust, Buber refused to give one. "If Buber *had* given one," I pointed out, "he would have negated everything he stood for." Existential trust can never be equated with a theology or world-view. It is at best a Dialogue with the Absurd. Emil Fackenheim (whom I regard as the greatest living Jewish theologian) forgets this when he reproaches Buber, from the vantage of forty years later, for not following in Fackenheim's own footsteps and constructing a philosophy or theology that takes the Holocaust into account. I can do no better than quote from the ending of "The Dialogue between Heaven and Earth," the third of the speeches that Buber gave when he first lectured in New York in 1951:

> How is a life with God still possible in a time in which there is an Oswiecim [Auschwitz]? The estrangement has become too cruel, the hiddenness too deep. One can still "believe" in the God who allowed those things to happen, but can one still speak to Him? Can one still hear His word? Can one still, as an individual and as a people, enter at all into a dialogic relationship with Him? Can one still call to Him? Dare we recommend to the survivors of Oswiecim, the Job of the gas chambers: "Call to Him, for He is kind, for His mercy endurest forever"? . . . Nothing is explained, nothing adjusted; wrong has not become right, nor cruelty kindness. Nothing has happened but that man again hears God's address.
>
> The mystery has remained unsolved, but it has become his, it has become man's.
>
> And we?
>
> We—by that is meant all those who have not got over what happened and will not get over it. How is it with us? Do we stand overcome before the hidden face of God as the tragic hero of the Greeks before faceless fate? No, rather even now we contend, we

too, with God, even with Him, the Lord of Being, Whom we once, we here, chose for our Lord. We do not put up with earthly being, we struggle for its redemption, and struggling we appeal to the help of our Lord, Who is again and still a hiding one. In such a state we await His voice whether it come out of the storm or out of a stillness which follows it. Though His coming appearance resemble no earlier one, we shall recognize again our cruel and merciful Lord.[10]

Primo Levi

A few years ago, when I was lecturing on Elie Wiesel during the week devoted to the *Shoah* at the Jewish Community Center in San Diego, I spoke of Primo Levi, who, we had been told, killed himself in 1987. During the discussion a member of the audience asked me why Primo Levi had committed suicide and Elie Wiesel had not. I responded, of course, that this is an impossible question which no one would presume to answer. The shocking news of Levi's death in 1987 was still fresh in our minds. When I spoke to Elie about it, he remarked that Levi was a chemist and could have done it painlessly instead of throwing himself down a stairwell. But, he added, "They take Primo Levi to have had a psychological problem when actually it was a metaphysical one."

Now that I have read in Ferdinando Camon's *Conversations with Primo Levi* about the letter Levi wrote Camon two days before his death, I find it still more remarkable that a man so involved with plans for the future committed suicide. But apart from this, his suicide can hardly cancel out a lifetime of writing that again and again transcended the horror and trauma that he experienced during his year in Auschwitz without ever leaving it behind. A statement "About the Author" at the end of Levi's last book, *The Drowned and the Saved*, reads:

> Primo Levi's luminous writings offer a wondrous celebration of life. His universally acclaimed books remain a testament to the indomitability of the human spirit and mankind's capacity to defeat death through meaningful work, morality and art.[11]

Apart from the fact that he killed himself, Levi did not deny the absurd and he did not succumb to it. Rather, he engaged in a lifelong Dialogue with the Absurd through which he found not only the meaning of his own life, but also the meaning of our times and of human history and human existence in general. Something of his spirit is indicated by Ferdinando Camon at the end of his preface to his conversations:

> Levi did not shout, did not assail, did not accuse, because he didn't *want* to shout. He wanted something much more: to *make* people shout. He renounced his own reaction in exchange for the reaction of the rest of us. He took a long-range view. His mildness, his gentleness, his smile—which had something shy, almost childlike about it—were actually his weapons.[12]

Our theme of affirming in the midst of withstanding is a deliberately paradoxical concept. It affirms meaning, but it also asserts the absurd and leaves meaning and the absurd in tension with each other. The significance of this paradox may perhaps emerge more clearly if we contrast it with Viktor Frankl's famous watchword "the search for meaning," to which we have already alluded in our Introduction. Frankl's assertion that it is *always* possible to find meaning gives meaning a universal status that divorces it from the very existential and unique situations that Frankl claims give rise to it. There is no room left for the Absurd or the Dialogue with the Absurd.

Frankl is fond of quoting Nietzsche's saying that any *how* can be borne where there is a *why*. In his first book, *Survival in Auschwitz*, Primo Levi tells of how one day as an inmate in this death camp he reached out his hand for an icicle outside the window to slake his unbearable thirst. A guard came by just then and knocked the icicle down so that Levi could not get it. "Why?" the anguished Levi cried out. *"Hier ist kein Warum."*—"Here there is no Why," the guard responded.

It is precisely this confrontation with meaninglessness that one finds in every page of Elie Wiesel and Primo Levi and that I find missing in Frankl. In my critique of Frankl's psychology of religion I write:

> This is . . . part of [Frankl's] focus on the hero and the saint that makes him give his attention to the few who were able to preserve their "inner liberty" and find meaning in suffering. From this Frankl turned his search for meaning not only into an approach to therapy but also into a philosophical dogma. Otherwise he would not be able to assert that meaning is always possible in every situation. Job's question has no place in Frankl's world nor the way in which Job contended even in the midst of his trust.[13]

Survival in Auschwitz is a remarkably detailed, concrete recounting interspersed with pointed philosophical observations about life in the *Lager,* or camp, such as the lesson that Levi had to learn hurriedly once he was there: "man is bound to pursue his own ends by all possible means, while he who errs but once pays dearly." Unlike condemned prisoners, these inmates were granted no comfort or solitude before being killed: "Night came, and it was such a night that one knew that human eyes would not witness it and survive." None of the Italian or German guards "had the courage to come and see what men do when they know they have to die." Yet mothers fed their children. "Would you not do the same?" Levi asks the reader. With dawn came collective, uncontrolled panic; happy memories of home were as painful as sword thrusts. "Many things were then said and done among us; but of these it is better that there remain no memory."

In one chapter Levi narrates the story of Lorenzo, a "good and simple" Italian civilian worker who brought him bread and rations every day for six months without any thought of reward. Lorenzo saved Levi's life because he preserved for him an image of the human amidst its universal destruction. For most civilians the prisoners were untouchables, tainted by some mysterious grave sin, untrustworthy animals and thieves, muddy, ragged, and starving, worthy of their abasement. Lorenzo, in contrast, constantly reminded Levi by his presence and his simple manner of being good "that there still existed a just world outside our own," a remote possibility of good for which it was worth surviving. I cannot imagine a simpler and more profound denial of our nothingness, a more effective discovery of meaning in the midst of the confrontation with death, evil, and the absurd:

> The personages in these pages are not men. Their humanity is buried . . . under an offense received or inflicted on someone else. The evil and insane SS men, the Kapos, the politicals, the criminals, the prominents, great and small, down to the indifferent slave *Häftlinge*, all the grades of the mad hierarchy created by the Germans paradoxically fraternize in a uniform internal desolation.
>
> But Lorenzo was a man; his humanity was pure and uncon-

taminated, he was outside this world of negation. Thanks to Lorenzo, I managed not to forget that I myself was a man.[14]

Before Elie Wiesel or any other writer on the *Shoah* had commented on the impossibility of ever communicating in ordinary language the reality of the death camp, Levi recognized that a new, harsh language would have to emerge to "express what it means to toil the whole day in the wind, with the temperature below freezing, wearing only a shirt, underpants, cloth jacket and trousers, and in one's body nothing but weakness, hunger and knowledge of the end drawing nearer."[15] If Lorenzo helped Levi deny our human nothingness, it did not mean any denial on Levi's part of the nothingness that stood at the very center of the *Lager,* where everything is nothing, "except the hunger inside and the cold and the rain around."

Even the man who is hanged by the Nazis after taking part in a revolt and who cries out, "Comrades, I am the last one!" only mirrors for Primo Levi and his friend Alberto how emptied they are of violence, defiance, or even judgment. The man who is hanged was made of a different metal, for the condition which could not bend him broke and conquered them "even if we have finally learnt how to find our food and to resist the fatigue and cold, even if we return home." Perhaps the only remnant of their humanity is the fact that after they satisfy the daily ragings of hunger, they are oppressed by shame. Only when the *Lager* is dead is it conceivable to offer a slice of bread to others in defiance of the law of the *Lager* that said: "eat your own bread, and, if you can, that of your neighbor." The existence of Auschwitz makes it impossible to speak of Providence in our age, Levi reflects. The only thing that is providential is the natural law which, when suffering passes a certain limit, dulls that sensitivity which is a source of pain.

Yet if Providence cannot exist for Levi after Auschwitz, the human can and does, and it becomes for him the source of a judgment that would have been unthinkable when he was totally immersed in the *Lager*:

> It is man who kills, man who creates or suffers injustice; it is no longer man who, having lost all restraint, shares his bed with a corpse. Whoever waits for his neighbor to die in order to take his piece of bread is, albeit guiltless, further from the model of thinking man than the most primitive pygmy or the most vicious sadist.[16]

Levi's final witness is the gratitude and friendship he feels for the companions whose shared feelings enabled all three of them to remain largely immune to that nonhuman experience of living through months during which man is merely a thing in the eyes of man.

In *The Reawakening*, the story of his long journey home, Levi tells of how finally, after untold hardships, time regained its vigor and value and "was once more working for us." When they reached the soil of Germany itself, they felt an urgent need to settle accounts with every single German as to whether they knew and how they faced the silent daily massacre occurring a step away from their doors. "I felt the tattooed number on my arm burning like a sore," says Levi, but the Germans, still imprisoned in their fortress of willful ignorance, hatred, and contempt, did not feel it. Returning home to Turin in Italy, he is visited again and again by a dream full of horror in which his peaceful surroundings give way to chaos and he is alone in the center of a grey and turbid nothing. He is in the *Lager* and nothing else is real but the command "*Wstawach* (get up)."

172

In the afterword to *The Reawakening* Levi answers the questions that recurred again and again among his readers. Hatred and desire for revenge are not in his temperament, and even the temptation to hatred and violence that would arise if he saw "certain old faces, certain old lies" he would overcome. To direct hatred at all the Germans as an ethnic group would be to follow the Nazis. But this does not mean that he has forgiven or is ready to forgive a single one of the Italian fascists and German Nazis unless they have shown by deeds, not too long afterward, that they condemn their earlier crimes and want to uproot them. In particular Levi indicts the German people who, on the whole, were fully culpable of deliberately *not* knowing the "final solution" and not making it known.

Both the Italians and the Germans followed with adoration their charismatic leaders and diligently executed their inhuman orders. Therefore, Levi rejects charismatic leaders and regards all prophets with suspicion:

> It is better to content oneself with other more modest and less exciting truths, those one acquires painfully, little by little and without shortcuts, with study, discussion, and reasoning, those that can be verified and demonstrated.[17]

Consonant with all of the above is Levi's deliberate assumption of a calm, objective, reportorial tone in his writings to prepare the ground for the judges, his readers. It was Levi's writing itself that gave him the incentive to live and carry on his lifelong task of affirming in the midst of withstanding. Of this task as writer-witness, Levi himself says that the sum total is clearly positive. Not only has the past made him richer and surer; it has taught him many things about man and the world. Above all, it has taught him how to snatch meaning from the heart of evil and absurdity:

I was also helped by the determination, which I stubbornly preserved, to recognize always, even in the darkest days, in my companions and in myself, men, not things, and thus to avoid that total humiliation and demoralization which led so many to spiritual shipwreck.[18]

This is a witness to the human that goes far beyond that rational verification and demonstration to which Levi the scientist points!

Nellie Sachs and Paul Celan

In his 1963 introduction to Nelly Sachs's selected English poems *O the Chimneys*, Hans Magnus Enzensberger writes:

> In her Stockholm refuge she [Nelly Sachs] experienced the genocide of the Final Solution more closely than we who lived near the death camps, and her book remains the only poetic testimony that can hold its own beside the dumbfounding horror of the documentary reports.[19]

At the beginning of the Second World War Sachs managed to escape to Stockholm. In her own postscript to *Eli: A Mystery Play of the Sufferings of Israel* (Time: "After Martyrdom"), Sachs testifies to the central impact of the Holocaust on her life and work and, permeated by the spirit of Martin Buber's *Tales of the Hasidim*, to the equally central importance of Hasidism and the Kabbalah:

> In his world of night, where a secret equilibrium seems to reign, the victim is always innocence. . . .

This mystery play was the outcome of a terrible experience of the Hitler time at the height of its smoke and flame, and was written down in a few nights after my flight to Sweden.

The shepherd's pipe raised in desperation by a child to God—attempted outbreak of the human in the face of horror. . . .

No more trust in good on earth.

Written in a rhythm which must make the Hassidic mystical fervor visible also in mime to the performer—the encounter with the divine radiance which accompanies each of our everyday words. Always designed to raise the unutterable to a transcendental level, so as to make it bearable and in this night of nights to give a hint of the holy darkness in which quiver and arrow [Deutero-Isaiah's suffering servant of the Lord] is hidden.[20]

"O the Chimneys," the title poem of the English selected poems, is also the lead poem of the selections from Sachs's first collection, *In the Habitations of Death.* In this poem the chimneys themselves are "the ingeniously devised habitations of death / When Israel's body drifted as smoke / Through the air," and they are the "Freedomway for Jeremiah and Job's dust / . . . The road for refugees of smoke." It is they that lay the threshold "Like a knife between life and death." The knife and dust are two of Nelly Sachs's repeated themes. When she asks in another poem "who emptied your shoes of sand / When you had to get up to die?" she links it to Israel's nomad burning Sinai sand and foretells that those fingers "that emptied the deathly shoes of sand," tomorrow will be dust in the shoes of those to come.[21]

In one poem of this collection Sachs offers us an obscure intimation of redemption when the last breaths and eyelids' good night of old men that "you thieves of genuine hours of death" snatched away are gathered by the "angel" into a wind that shall "drive this unloosed star / Into its Lord's hands!" On the other hand, when she asks what secret cravings of the blood brought into being Hitler, "the terrible puppeteer" "with foaming mouth" who turned "the setting sun of Sinai's people" into "A red carpet [of blood] under their feet," she offers us no breath of hope but only "on the ash-gray receding horizon of fear / Gigantic the constellation of death / That loomed like the clock face of ages."[22]

In Elie Wiesel's novel *The Town beyond the Wall*, Michael discovers that he has been impelled to return to his native city by the desire to find the man who watched impassively from the square above during the whole week in which the Jews of the city were gathered in the synagogue and deported to their deaths. The spectator's "presence is evasive, and commits him less than his absence might. . . . He is there, but he acts as if he were not. Worse: he acts as if the rest of us were not." He reduces himself and us to the level of objects. Nelly Sachs confronts this same theme in her poem "You Onlookers" "Whose eyes watched the killing. / As one feels a stare at one's back" "who raised no hand in murder, / But who did not shake the dust / From your longing,/ You who halted there, where dust is changed / To light."[23]

In one of her later collections of poetry, *Death Still Celebrates Life*, Sachs offers us an enigmatic poem which fuses the horror of Holocaust death with a strange transcendence, picturing a room in which is preserved "the smile of the child / who was thrown as in play / into playing flames" of the Nazi bonfires (an act which Elie Wiesel witnessed as soon as he arrived at the death camps). "I know," concludes the poet, "that this is the food / from which earth with beating heart / ignites the music of her stars—" The reader cannot fathom what redemption is presaged here, yet the tone seems in no way ironic.

It is no accident that the last three sections of poems in this volume are titled "Glowing Enigmas." In the first such poem Sachs pictures herself turning the corner into a dark side street, where-

176

upon her shadow lay down in her arm, a "tired piece of clothing" that "wanted to be carried." Here the transcendence pushes us to the utmost limit, as in Karl Jaspers's notion of "shipwreck": "the color Nothing addressed me:/ *You are beyond!*" We do not have here a Whiteheadian optimism in which God preserves all things of time in a process which, with infinite slowness, turns evil to good. Rather we have "empty time" which "is hungry / for the inscription of transitoriness," and we who are "furled into night's banner" with all its marvels "know nothing / save that your loneliness / is not mine"—a note worthy of Nelly Sachs's friend Paul Celan. Yet even so in a dream or a song from prebirth "from the bridges of sighs of our speech [the "bridge of sighs" over which prisoners condemned to solitude or death in Renaissance Venice walked to their doom] / we hear the secret roar of the deeps."[24]

Paul Celan was a Rumanian Jew who lived the post–World War II years in Paris until his suicide in 1970. Originally he wrote in Rumanian and then in German. The news of the execution of his mother by the Nazis in 1943 left a deep imprint on Celan's life. This is expressed directly in only a few of his poems but indirectly in most.

"Death Fugue" from *Mohn und Gedächtnis* (*Poppy and Rememberance*) (1952) is Paul Celan's most famous and most anthologized poem, and it is also the one that deals most explicitly with the *Shoah* with its repeated motif of Jews digging their own graves and the repeated contrast between "golden hair Margarete and ashen hair Shulamith":

death is a master from Germany his eyes are blue
he strikes you with leaden bullets his aim is true . . .
he sets his pack on to us he grants us a grave in the air
he plays with the serpents and daydreams death is a master
    from Germany[25]

Far more often Celan's reference to the *Shoah* is subtle, as in his long poem *"Engführung"* ("Straitening") from *Sprachgitter* (1959), which begins with "the unmistakable track," continues with grass, stones, wheel, blackish field, "the night that needs no stars, nowhere anyone asking after you, ash, gales, silence, poison, a crafty sky, whirl of particles," "the world, a millicrystal, shot up," "nights, demixed," "no smoke soul ascends or joins in," "the rifle range near the buried wall: visible, once more: the grooves," "nothing is lost," and ends as it began with:

> Driven into the
> terrain
> with
> the unmistakable
> track:
>
> Grass.
>
> Grass,
>
> written asunder.[26]

Another poem "Think of It," from *Fadensonnen* (1968) fuses two events two millennia apart—the last resistance of Bar Kochba and the Jews to the Romans at the beginning of the Common Era and the first (and only possible) resistance of the inmates of an early Nazi concentration camp in the form of its famous song of "Die Moorsoldaten," or peat bog soldiers.[27]

"Celan's was the silence of the unutterable, his exile a flight from the unforgivable," writes Katharine Washburn in close consonance with Martin Buber's central image of the "eclipse of God."[28] "The anguish, the darkness, the shadow of death are present in all his work, early and late," writes Michael Hamburger, "including the most high-spirited and sensuous." This applies not only to the content of Celan's poetry but also to his very way of writing it. If Celan described his poems as "ways of a voice to a receptive you," a "desperate dialogue," and "a sort of home-coming," this did not gainsay the fact that his poetry was rooted in "extreme experience that could not be enacted in any manner less difficult than his. The hiatuses, the silences, the dislocations of normal usage belong to what he had to say and to the effort of saying it."[29]

Hamburger points to negation as a recurrent theme of Celan's later poetry in general, linking it to Jewish and Christian mysticism and to the dialectic of light and darkness that runs all through Celan's work. What is striking about Celan's poetry is that he holds the tension, keeping yes and no unsplit, thereby admitting enough darkness into his poems to remain true to his own dictum that "he speaks truly who speaks the shade."[30]

The theme of "There was Earth Inside Them" (from *Die Nie-mandsrose*, 1963) is the constantly reiterated digging that links the poem to "The Death Fugue" as does the statement, "they did not praise God, / who, so they heard, wanted all this, / who, so they heard, knew all this." The suggestion of the absurdity and futility of everything is strengthened by the line, "I dig, you dig, and the worm digs too" and by the question, "Where did the way lead when it led nowhere?" Yet behind all this there is at least some minimal contact of I and Thou: "O you dig and I dig, and I dig towards you, / and on our finger the ring awakes."[31] "There was Earth Inside Them" compels us to think of the eclipse of God. A God who hears and knows all this and wants it to happen, as Celan writes, is an indifferent God, a monstrous God. The God who cares about us is in eclipse.

In "Zurich, the Stork Inn" from the same volume, the Thou becomes explicit in Celan's dedication of the poem to Nelly Sachs, whom he met at this place. At this inn Nelly Sachs had a mystic experience of the light of the sun, which Celan shared. But Celan was still struggling with this "Jewish God" in the depths of his being: "Of your God was our talk, I spoke / against him, I / let the heart that I had / hope: / for / his highest, death-rattled, his / quarreling word— / Your eye looked on, looked away, / your mouth / spoke its way to the eye, and I heard."[32] This does not mean that Celan denied God. Yet for him God was more profoundly in eclipse than for Sachs. In 1959 in one of the many Buber books that he was always buying and reading, Celan underlined, "Every name is a step toward the consummate Name, as everything broken points to the unbroken," and twice he noted Buber's words, "All of time is immediate to redemption." On the other hand, on hearing Nelly Sachs's "Yes, I'm a believer," Celan replied that he hoped to "blaspheme to the end" after which she repeated his statement, "One really doesn't know what counts."[33] Celan's "addressable Thou" is also a problematic Thou. "Celan turns most Jewish in struggling with Jewish faith," comments Felstiner.[34]

Something similar is echoed in "So Many Constellations." Although we are told of Time which stands in that chasm where extinguished things "splendid with teats" stood, "Time / on which already grew up / and down and away all that / is or was or will be," nonetheless Celan concludes with an affirmation of the dialogue. Although "we / don't know, do we? / what / counts," still at times when only "das Nichts [the Void] stood between us we got / all the way to each other."[35]

Hamburger locates Celan's religion precisely in the task of coming to grips with his experience of being God-forsaken, with the negation and blasphemy through which alone Celan could be true to his own experience "and yet maintain the kind of intimate dialogue with God characteristic of Jewish devotion."[36]

We need only think of Abraham, Job, Levi Yitzhak of

Berditchev, Martin Buber, and Elie Wiesel to understand the protest of what I call the "Job of Auschwitz" to which Celan, too, belongs. This is made explicit in the poem Celan wrote after his visit with Nelly Sachs at the Stork Inn in Zurich in 1960. When Celan speaks in that poem, as we have seen, of God's "death-rattled, his quarreling word," Celan's German original for "quarreling" is "*haderndes*," the word used in the German translation of the Hebrew Bible, when Job urged God, "Make me know wherefore Thou contendest with me" (Job 20:2). Celan's very defiance bred assertion. "Bitter yes," Celan said, but he added, "In what's truly bitter, there is surely the More-than-bitter."[37] It is precisely this combination of dialogue, or trust, and contending that I point to again and again when I speak of the biblical Job, the "Modern Job," and "the Job of Auschwitz."

In "Your/ being beyond," from *The No One's Rose,* Celan repeats the kabbalistic lore that God is split into two parts—the *Ein Sof,* or transcendent infinite, and the *Shekinah,* the part that is scattered in exile. "In the death / of all those mown down," claims the poet, God "grows himself whole." He also claims that "with this / half / we keep up relations," "this half" presumably being the scattered one. Perhaps in the language of the Kabbalah we could say that Celan shared the anguish and suffering of God's exile.

The "Psalm" from this same volume is also the origin of the title; for it is "No One" who "moulds us again out of earth and clay" and "conjures our dust," and for whose sake "we shall flower toward you . . . the No One's rose." "We bloom in thy sight, in thy spite," reads Felstiner's translation of the poem. This Nothing and No One could be the Jewish God, the primordial Nothing, of the Kabbalah. But it could equally well be God in eclipse. It expresses perfectly Celan's vacillation, his standing in the tension between affirmation and negation. In "Conversation in the Mountains" the

Jew Klein also speaks to and is heard by No One. "In that story and this poem," comments Felstiner, "the absent 'No One' of the catastrophe [the *Shoah*] masks the unknowable 'No One' of Jewish mysticism." "A Nothing / we were, are now, and ever shall be," reads "Psalm." This *Ein Nichts*, asserts Felstiner, "again merges mystical with historical nothingness."[38]

"What Occurred?" carries similar overtones of the kabbalistic Book of Creation, of darkness and light, heaviness and lightness, of the awakening of I and Thou, and of the intrinsic relation between language, "co-earth," and "fellow planet."[39] We might think here of the kabbalistic legend according to which God hewed the letters out of stone, weighed them, switched them around until he found the right order, and only then created the world.[40]

Celan's vacillation is again seen in "Thread Suns" (*Atemwende*, 1967) where we find whatever stands above the Ödnis, "the grey-black wilderness"—the mind that transcends it with "tree-high thought," "tunes in to light's pitch" or whatever comes after it—some afterlife or even life on this earth in which "there are/ still songs to be sung on the other side / of mankind." Nor is the tension of this vacillation any less in Celan's very latest poems, as in "I hear that the axe has flowered" (*Schneepart*, 1971). The axe that has flowered is both instrument of destruction and construction. The hanged man is healed by the bread his wife baked for him, the bread which looks at him. "I hear that the place can't be named." People don't talk about the Holocaust any more. We plant flowers in all the places where the death camps were. "I hear that they call life / our only refuge," the poem concludes, possibly referring to those who tell Jews to live in the present not the past, or possibly saying that there is no hope in or after death.[41]

Others of Celan's latest poems can only deepen what we have seen before, as in:

> World to be stuttered by heart
> in which
> I shall have been a guest, a name
> sweated down from the wall
> a wound licks up.[42]

A prompter from a cosmic theater helps us to learn the world by heart, but what we can learn, what we can know and live, is only a stuttering. We live in the face of the memorial wall in which the image of the flame sweated down is complemented by that of the wound licking up. Again in "A Leaf," Celan parodies Brecht's criticism of those who do not speak out, inverting a leafless tree into a treeless leaf as a prelude to "What times are these / when a conversation / is almost a crime / because it includes / so much made explicit?" Except for the "Death Fugue," Celan felt he could not and did not want to speak explicitly. Correspondingly, in "I Fool About" the shadows belong to the truth as well as the light, the shadows which are the echo of what happened in the past, heard "from every direction, / the incontrovertible echo / of every eclipse." We cannot help thinking here of Buber's "eclipse of God" to which, as Elie Wiesel has stated, not only the Jews but all mankind became subject when the Nazi regime plunged the world into the Night. But here, too, the note of dialogue is present: "your darkness too / load on to / my halved, voyaging / eyes."[43]

Thus Celan walks the "narrow ridge" between the abysses in which Nothing is at one and the same time the absurd and the divine Nothing of the Kabbalah. In "Hour of the Barge," one of his last poems, Celan speaks of being "rid of death, rid of God." In "To Speak with Blind Alleys" he writes of speaking about what we might call variously the partner, the vis-à-vis, the face to face, "about its expatriate meaning" (Celan's own exile, the exile of the Jews, the exile of the *Shekinah*), "to chew the bread with writing teeth." In "Hail of Stones" Celan describes one who stood fast in his despair and succeeded in far-striding silence. With all of this, he searches continually for his Thou, who is at the same time the eternal Thou, as in "Shot Forth" ("Shot forth / in the emerald race, / hatching of grubs, hatching of stars, with every / keel / I search for you [*dich*], / fathomless"). In "My Soul" his soul inclines toward his Thou, "hears you thundering," learns to sink itself "in the pit of your throat" and "become true." When the unkissed stone of grief stirs in its fulfillment, Celan says in "We, Who Were True Like the Bent Grass," "it changes over to us," and "we hand ourselves on"; "to you and to me," with whom ("watch out"!) the night is painstaking.[44]

In Celan's 1969 poem "Nothingness" ("Das Nichts") the eclipse of God stands forth with all possible clarity. "Nothingness [*das Nichts*], for our name's sake / they gather us in—. / sets a seal, / the end believes we're / the beginning, / in front of / masters / going silent around us, / in the Undivided, there testifies / a binding brightness."[45] Felstiner's comment on this poem, which he himself translates, again evokes the eclipse of God and the tension in Celan between affirmation and negation: "A strange ingathering occurs. Instead of God guiding us in straight paths 'for His name's sake,' it is Nothingness—*a presence both ineffable and eclipsed* [italics mine] for *our* names' sake."[46]

On Celan's suicide itself Felstiner speculates that perhaps Celan felt too alone ("No one / witnesses for the / witness"). Speaking from his deathbed in America a month later, the intellectual historian Erich Kahler ascribed Celan's suicide to "the terrible psychic burden—the burden of being both a great German poet and a young Central European Jew growing up in the shadow of the concentration camps."[47]

Celan does not represent any tradition. He does not stand within any community, not even that of Israel, nor, for all of his attachment to the Kabbalah, Hasidism, and Buber, was he the spokesman for any tradition the way Eliot was for Catholic Christianity. His very existence as a Rumanian Jewish survivor of the Nazi camps living in Paris and writing in German left Celan forever in exile. True to what he and his contemporaries had experienced, Celan could not offer a comfortable mirror of a less fragmented, less ambiguous, less absurd, or less eclipsed existence.

Conclusion

Confronting Death

Finding meaning in the lived concrete, encountering evil, and going through and beyond the absurd to affirming in the midst of withstanding—all these place us squarely before the centrality of death in human existence. We need look no further than the poetry of Emily Dickinson, discussed in chapter 4, to find a particularly vivid example of this. The hero of Tolstoy's great story "The Death of Ivan Ilyich" screams at the top of his lungs for the week before he dies because his awareness that he is dying also confronts him with the emptiness and inauthenticity of his unlived life.

The human being is the only creature who knows that he will die and who makes of this knowledge a foundation for his life and even for his *joie de vivre*.

For the *Upanishads* the knowledge of death leads to the choice of the good over the pleasant; for the Buddha it leads to overcoming the craving for existence and to the eightfold path to nirvana; for Greek tragedy it leads to reconciliation with *moira*, the qualitative order that includes man, even when, as with Oedipus, "one dare not count one's lot as gain until the last breath is drawn without pain." For Lao-tzu death is no threat to life, since both are a part of the flowing of the Tao. For Psalm 90 the knowledge that all flesh is as the grass which grows up in the morning and withers in the evening leads to a desire, not to escape from the mutable to the immutable, as with Plato, but to "number our days so that we may get a heart of wisdom." For Ecclesiastes the fact of death merges with the passing of all things in time and grows to an impassioned cry to remember your Creator in the days of your youth before desire fails, the grasshopper drags itself along, the silver cord is loosed, the golden bowl broken at the cistern, and all the daughters of song laid low.

Only in the book of Job does the human condition of death lead to outright rebellion: "Consider that my days are as a breath." "My sons will come to grief, and I will know it not." "Thou wilt seek me, and I shall not be." "It is all one, I despise my life. Therefore, I say, He mocks at the calamity of the guiltless. If it be not He, who then is it?"

Even "when the last Red Man shall have perished and the memory of his tribe [is] just a myth among the White Men, these shores will swarm with the invisible dead of my tribe," said Chief Seattle. So far from there being places dedicated to solitude, even at nighttime the seemingly deserted streets of the White Man's cities and villages "will throng with the returning hosts that once filled them and still love this beautiful land." Seattle's final words are a stunning confession of his faith: "Dead, did I say? There is no death, only a change of worlds."[1] There is a striking parallel here to the Hasidic view of death, as I have described it in "The World of Death" chapter of my book *A Dialogue with Hasidic Tales*:

A Hasid of Rabbi Menahem Mendel of Vorki reported the death of a zaddik as "very beautiful. It was as though he went from one room into the next." "No, from one corner of the room into another corner," rejoined Rabbi Mendel. When the Baal Shem died, he said, "I have no worries with regard to myself. For I know quite clearly: I am going out at one door and I shall go in at another." "Man is always passing through two doors," said Rabbi Bunam: "out of this world and into the next, and out and in again." "Death is merely moving from one home to another," said the Kotzker rebbe. "If we are wise, we will make the latter the more beautiful home."[2]

Something of the Native American attitude toward death is embodied in Margaret Craven's novel *I Heard the Owl Call My Name,* which is a faithful evocation of Indian life and spirit at Kingcome Village, British Columbia. The Indian of this village feels for it as no white man for his country, town, or even his own bit of land.

> The myths are the village and the winds and the rains. The river is the village, and the black and white killer whales that herd the fish to the end of the inlet the better to gobble them. The village is the . . . talking bird, the owl, who calls the name of the man who is going to die.[3]

The young vicar, who, the bishop is told by the doctor, is going to die within two years, is sent by the bishop to the Indian villages in Kingcome for what the bishop knows will be a hard but meaningful work of ministry.

When the mark of death is visible on Mark's face, one of the elder Indian women fulfills her promise to the bishop and writes him that the time has come. The bishop comes in person to the village. "Always when I leave the village I try to define what it means to me," the bishop says to Mark. He cannot put it into words, he adds, but when he reaches it, he knows that for him it has always been easier in the village where the fundamentals count, to learn what every man must learn in this world: "enough of the meaning of life to be ready to die." This statement is remarkably similar to what the Hasidic rabbi Bunam says to his wife when he is dying and she bursts into tears: "What are you crying for? My whole life was only that I might learn how to die."[4]

Martin Buber planned to have a chapter on death in his philosophical anthropology, *The Knowledge of Man,* but then decided against it because, as he told me, we do not know death in itself as we know the concrete realities of our existence. This is true, but what we do know is the anticipation of death—the imagining of death—our own and others, and the attitude one brings to this somber and unavoidable future. Buber himself in his early mystical work *Daniel* saw death not just as the movement of past to future but of future to past, and the two so intertwined that death permeated life at every moment:

How could I become death's if I had not already now suffered it? My existence . . . was the bed in which two streams, coming from opposite directions, flowed to and in and over each other. There was not only in me a force that moved from the point of birth to the point of death or beyond; there was also a counterforce from death to birth, and each moment that I experienced as a living man had grown out of the mixture of the two. . . . A force bore me toward dying, and its flight I called time; but in my face blew a strange wind, and I did not know what name to give its flight. . . . Coming-to-be and passing-away . . . lay side by side in endless embrace, and each of my moments was their bed. It was foolish to wish to limit death to any particular moments of ceasing to be or of transformation; it was an ever-present might and the mother of being. Life engendered being, death received and bore it; life scattered its fullness, death preserved what it wished to retain.[5]

The director of Insel Verlag, which published both Buber and Rilke, sent Buber's *Daniel* to Rilke, who liked it very much. To the Rilke of the *Duino Elegies* and the *Sonnets to Orpheus* death was a central concern, and in a manner not unlike Buber's *Daniel* death and life formed together one reality for Rilke. This becomes radiantly clear if we look at the full last stanza of the Ninth Elegy, a part of which we cited earlier:

> Earth, isn't this what you want: an invisible
> re-arising in us? Is it not your dream
> to be one day invisible? Earth! invisible!
> What is your urgent command, if not transformation?
> Earth, you darling, I will! Oh, believe me, you need
> your Springs no longer to win me: a single one,
> just one, is already more than my blood can endure.
> I've now been unspeakably yours for ages and ages.
> You were always right, and your holiest inspiration's
> Death, that friendly Death.
> Look, I am living. On what? Neither childhood nor future
> are growing less . . . Supernumerous existence
> wells up in my heart.[6]

Rilke calls death "friendly" because he sees life and death, the visible and the invisible as a seamless whole.

The human attitude toward death has always been bound up in the closest way with the human posture vis-à-vis nature, time, and community. Although he is aware of the seasons, the modern hardly lives in the time of nature. His time is abstract, calendrical, and conventional, and his relations to nature are more and more detached— whether nature be the object to be exploited, the scene to rhapsodize over, the terrain for a holiday from the city, or the great Earth Goddess celebration every year on Earth Day to ward off the threat of pollution and ecological imbalance. One recent book entitled *The End of Nature*[7] signifies that we no longer even possess a nature that is truly other than we are. This does not mean that we are closer to nature but that we have lost contact with real nature altogether because we have robbed it of its otherness and made it over in our image. As a result it is hardly possible for us moderns to see our own death as a part of the natural rhythms and cycles of nature, to be accepted with the wisdom of nature itself.

The awareness of past and future is an inextricable part of all living in the present. The people living in the age of Jesus already needed to be told to live in the present and not sell it short for the sake of the imagined tomorrow. But only for us moderns has presentness been thoroughly emptied of meaning. Only our relation to the present has become so technicized—so much the effect of a past cause or the means to a future end—that Pascal's dictum that we must be forever unhappy knowing no real present is plain to all who pause for a moment in the unending rush. "The world is too much with us; late and soon, / Getting and spending, we lay waste our powers," wrote Wordsworth. The death of T. S. Eliot's Sweeney is no tragedy because he has never known any meaningful life, and Eliot's Gerontion says, "Think at last / We have not reached conclusion, when I / Stiffen in a rented house."

To Melville, life means constant risk: man is out at sea in an open boat with harpoon lines whizzing around his head, threatening at any moment to carry him overboard to his death. To Eliot, the boat itself without the harpoon lines suffices, for death is certain in any case: "In a drifting boat with a slow leakage" man listens silently "to the undeniable / Clamor of the bell of the last annunciation." Every moment of our lives is a gradual submergence into death. Yet neither in our own lives, which have a beginning and end, nor in the beginningless, endless movement of time itself can we find a meaning:

192

We cannot think of a time that is oceanless
Or of an ocean not littered with wastage
Or of a future that is not liable
Like the past, to have no destination.

This is the thought we cannot face. To live as persons, we have to have a sense of meaning in our personal life and in history. Yet there is nowhere in time itself that meaning can be found. We are forever setting out on "a trip that will be unpayable / For a haul that will not bear examination." There is no end to "the drifting wreckage, / The bone's prayer to Death its God."[8]

Like K. in Kafka's novel *The Castle,* our attempt to find a foothold in present reality cannot succeed because we are always using the present as a means to some future end. This functional relation to time is caused in turn—and reinforced—by that sense of isolation, rootlessness, and exile which makes us feel, in moments of awareness, that we know no real life. We are cut off from the nourishing stream of community; the prospect of our own death takes on an overwhelming importance that robs life itself of meaning. This theme of isolation is endlessly repeated in modern literature: Thomas Hardy's hero Jude the Obscure, dying, deserted by everyone, with Job's curse on his lips; Camus's Meursault, the "stranger" who is aware of that slow wind blowing from the future that destroys all the false ideas of human brotherhood and solidarity that men put forward in the "unreal years" before death; Kafka's K. attaining a freedom greater than anyone has ever had— and equally meaningless; Jean-Paul Sartre's Matthieu, the hero of *The Age of Reason,* who is unable to belong to any person or group because he cannot commit himself or cherish any value beyond his own freedom.

Certainly, even in the best of communities, death is an individual affair. Even in traditional religions, the journey of the soul

193

to some Hades or Sheol must be facilitated by the community through *rites de passage*. Death *is* that uttermost solitude of which every other abandonment is only a foretaste, as Martin Buber suggests, and time is a torrent carrying us irreversibly and inexorably toward "the starkest of all human perspectives"—one's own death. But our obsession with our own deaths, our focus upon them, is in no small part caused by our exile and isolation in the present. This same obsession leads us to use our cults of youth, of having "experiences," of realizing our potentials, as ways of not looking at the facts of old age and death. Our culture gives us no support in hearing Gerard Manley Hopkins's "leaden echo" of old age in which we give up all the "girl-graces" of youth in favor of that vision in which every future is cut off except death. Yet this fear of time, old age, and death is woven into every moment of our existence, so that we have no real present and no real mutual presence for one another.

That which should be the very height of mutual presence—sex and love—has become the opposite. In *Love and Will* Rollo May has vividly shown how our culture uses sex as a way of not facing age or death, of pretending, with Mehitabel, that "there's life in the old gal yet," and that as long as we can go through some more or less adequate sexual functioning (itself endangered by our hurried relationship to time), we are still alive and not threatened by death.

Death is the Absurd precisely as Camus has defined it in *The Myth of Sisyphus*. It cuts us off from a meaningful relationship to past and future *and* from a meaningful relationship to each other. It is one thing to recognize with "Everyman" that no one else will go for you or that, like Jesus, "You gotta walk that lonesome valley, you gotta walk it by yourself." It is another to carry around one's general expectation and one's specific fears about death as an invisible barrier that gets in the way of any directness of relationship and of any present immediacy. How many of us can really say

194

with the Song of Songs, "For love is stronger than death," or with Martin Buber that "a great relationship throws a bridge across the abyss of dread of the universe," the abyss of death?

Death has always been the foremost advocate for the absurdity of life. "This too shall pass away." "All things change, all things perish, all things pass away." "Behold all flesh is as the grass and all the goodliness of man is as the flower of grass." "Vanity of vanities, all is vanity." It is death, as Bergson points out, that makes it necessary to supplement nature by habit and myth so that the depressing contingency which sunders present means and future end can be overlooked. But there is much in our day that has *heightened* the absurdity of death that we must confront to the point where it is qualitatively different.

The assassinations of John F. Kennedy and Martin Luther King Jr., the riots in Los Angeles, the Vietnam War and Desert Storm, and the Reagan-Bush systematic contribution to the killings on *both* sides in the ten-year war between Iran and Iraq have brought to the surface that terror and violence which seethe beneath the seemingly most successful civilization in the world's history. This is echoed throughout the world—Iraq's genocidal destruction of its Kurds; Bosnia's death camps for the "racially impure"; the growing racist violence in France, Germany, and Russia; and the systematic starvation of its people by the rival tribal chiefs of Somalia. Hiroshima, with its sudden death and long years of slow death by radiation, has created, as Robert Jay Lifton has shown, a "death-culture" in which even those who live are weighed down by the conviction that they, too, will be stricken, as well as by the "survivor guilt" of those who seem senselessly spared from a common doom. The atomic bomb survivors—*hibakusha*—"seem not only to have experienced the atomic disaster, but to have imbibed and incorporated it into their beings, including all of its elements of horror, evil, and particularly of death." Their own identities merge not only with dead relatives but with the anonymous dead. "With both Hiroshima and Nazi concentration camp survivors," writes Lifton, "the grotesqueness surrounding the death imprint . . . conveyed the psychological sense that death was not only everywhere, but was bizarre, unnatural, indecent, absurd." Even the seeming recovery of the atomic bomb victim became "a lifelong sense of vulnerability to the same grotesque death": His *jarring awareness of the fact of death* and his own mortality issued into a "vast breakdown of faith in the larger human matrix, and in the general structure of existence."[9] This death anxiety was not just concerned with dying itself, stresses Lifton, "but with *premature death and unfulfilled life.*"

> The *hibakusha* and the Nazi concentration camp survivor witnessed mass death that was awesome in its randomness, in its inclusion of small children quite new to life, and young adults at their prime, as well as old people who had in any case not much longer to live. The anxiety-laden imprint retained by both groups of survivors was of death that has *no reasonable relationship to life span or life cycle, of profoundly inappropriate death.*[10]

The grotesqueness and absurdity of the death imprint is exacerbated for the survivor of both types by the unconscious self-accusation "I am responsible for his death," which easily goes over into "I killed him," which in the concentration camp experience was sometimes literally true, from taking the other's food that he needed to keep alive to jostling people out of line when the selection for death was so random as odd and even, to selecting who lived and who died when one held the awesome and fearful position of *kapo.* None could be totally unaffected by a pervasive "either you or me" atmosphere, and it is this kind of death guilt which survivors of Nazi camps and Hiroshima refer to when they speak of their "living hell." Thus the original death imprint is complicated by a sense of continuous encounter with death, and death guilt is reinforced by group patterns within a "guilty community," and further reawakened, for the *hibakusha*, with every flexing of nuclear muscles—whether by words or testing—anywhere in the world.

Nor is this death guilt and death taint limited to the survivor alone. *We all share it.* "If only man knows that he will die," writes Lifton, "*only man could invent grotesquely absurd death. Only man through his technology, could render the meaningful totally meaningless.*" There is no longer any war-linked chivalry and glory or even a distinction between victimizer and victim, "only the sharing in species annihilation." "In every age man faces a pervasive theme which defies his engagement and yet must be engaged," writes Lifton in a remarkable anticipation of our theme of going through and beyond the absurd. In our day "it is unlimited technological violence and *absurd death.*"[11]

Hiroshima is not an isolated example: The Soviet Union's starvation of three million *Kulaks* in the vain effort to put through its communizing of agriculture in the 1930s, the bombing of civilian populations during the Second World War, the starvation of the children of Biafra, and the devastation in Indochina of millions of people by napalm, burning, bombing, disease, starvation, and outright murder—all these are illustration of the readiness of dictatorships and democracies alike in our day to create vast death cultures as instruments of national policy.

More than illustration—prototype—is the Nazi death camp in which six million Jews, one million gypsies, and four million other people were exterminated. "Auschwitz" stands not only for death and death culture, but for a systematic dehumanization such as the world had never known, a scientific undermining of the very foundations of social existence. In the world of Camus's *Plague* social and natural evil are one. In the world of Auschwitz social mistrust and existential mistrust are interwoven into the greatest assault on man as man that human history has known.

If we add to this the ever-present threat of a nuclear holocaust that might destroy all life on the planet and the predictions of the ecologists that the conditions for human life may disappear within forty, thirty, or even twenty years, we cannot avoid the conclusion that, however much death has challenged human meaning in the past, death for modern man is preeminently an encounter with the absurd.

In face of this situation, some persons revolt. One type of revolt against death in its aspect of the Absurd is that which in *Problematic Rebel* I call the "Modern Promethean." The Modern Promethean rebels against the very order of existence or against the absence of any order and does so in terms of the Either/Or of destroying what is over against one or being destroyed oneself. This heroic attitude toward death is a familiar one—from William Ernest Henley's "Invictus" ("I am the master of my fate, I am the captain of my soul") and Browning's "Prospice" ("I would not face death blindfold") to Dylan Thomas's "Do not go gentle into that goodnight. / Rage, rage against the dying of the light." Camus's Sisyphus rejects the possibility of suicide *despite* the absurdity of our relation to the irrational silence of the universe. Sisyphus' struggle to the heights with his everlasting rock is "enough to fill a man's heart," says the early Camus. This heroic stance takes on greater depth, as we have seen, with a character like Tarrou the journalist in Camus's novel *The Plague*—Tarrou, who has chosen to be victim rather than executioner, who has vowed never to assist in the murder of another even for the sake of the political party that represents the victims; Tarrou who perseveres in his revolt to the end in an awesome struggle against his own death.

Franz Rosenzweig, the modern Jewish existentialist philosopher and theologian, begins his *magnum opus, The Star of Redemption,*[12] by an attack on that "Philosophy of the All" which seeks to gloss over the fact that every creature awaits "the day of its journey into darkness with fear and trembling." Martin Heidegger makes the fact of individual death the cornerstone of his existentialist philosophy. Human existence is to Heidegger being-toward-death. It is only the resolute anticipation of one's unutterably unique and nonrelational death which individualizes our existence down to its own potentiality and frees it from the power of the crowd—the "They."

Jean-Paul Sartre rejects this cornerstone of Heidegger's philosophy on the ground that it is precisely in death that the person is abandoned to the *en-soi,* the objective in-itself, without any appeal left to that subjective personal becoming, or *pour-soi,* that during one's lifetime constantly transcends the facticity of what one is. But there is not only our anticipation of being turned into a thing, the revulsion against which filled even the martyr's death of Celia in T. S. Eliot's play *The Cocktail Party.* There is also our relationship to our own death, including that fact of finitude that gives concrete meaning to our existence—the precondition, says Paul Tillich in *Courage to Be,* of any enjoyment of positive being. The threat of "nonbeing," of contingency and death, is the given of our existence. But we have freedom in our relationship to that given because we are able to respond to it from our own ground.

Why then does Martin Buber (with special reference, I suspect, to his emphasis on death) speak of Martin Heidegger's philosophy as a "nightmare"? What Heidegger has left out, as Buber has argued in "What Is Man?"[13] is the ultimate reality of the interhuman—the realm between person and person. Similarly, the French Catholic existentialist Gabriel Marcel has maintained, in dialogue with Tillich and in explicit critique of Heidegger, that the death of the person who is my *Thou* is more real and important to me than my own death.

199

Granting that our anticipation of our death is a present reality that enters into every moment of our existence—and in this sense granting Heidegger's case over Sartre's—I would nonetheless hold that Heidegger takes the half-truth of separation that the knowledge of our unique and individual death imparts to each of us and makes it into the specious whole truth of our existence being "ultimately nonrelational." If the present moment of anticipation of death often gets in the way of our open presence to others, as I have suggested, it also constitutes the basis for genuine mutual presentness as opposed to any form of symbiotic clinging or ecstatic "unity." At its fullness this awareness of death in the present is far from being ultimately nonrelational. On the contrary, it is an integral part of the life of dialogue. It is the distancing that makes real the relating, the moving apart that makes real the moving together.

In this sense, I maintain—against both Heidegger and Camus's Meursault—that love *is* stronger than death. The anticipated reality of death is present in love and gives it its special poignancy without—when the love is real—destroying it.

Equally important, our existence is limitation and finitude even without our resolute anticipation of our individual death, as Sartre points out. Nor is its unique potentiality so bound up with this anticipation, as Heidegger holds. Our uniqueness is much more importantly connected with what calls us out in each hour and with such reality as we find in responding or failing to respond to that call. Our awareness of our death enters into both the situation and the response, but it does not dominate it. On the contrary, only when we are not *focusing* on the future negation of life by death do we have any presentness and immediacy. This does not gainsay the fact that we dare not deny the perhaps imminent reality of our own future death and the death of all we know and love.

We can understand the problematic of the Modern Promethean revolt against death better if we look at it in its somewhat less heroic and more clearly desperate form—suicide. If man is indeed the only creature that can commit suicide—which is not just the death of the body but the destruction of the self—man is also the only creature of which we know that has a "self" in any fully meaningful sense of that term. What is more, that self comes into being in the meeting with other selves. That self-preoccupation that makes suicide the only philosophical question of importance, as Camus claims in *The Myth of Sisyphus*, is mostly laid to one side in our actual lives, in which what is central is our response to what is not ourselves. Our self-realization is a *byproduct* of our meeting with other persons and beings in situations that include us rather than we them.

Leslie H. Farber has cogently asserted in *The Ways of the Will* that suicide, or "the life of suicide," is at its most basic a "willfulness" which refuses to accept the give-and-take of life, the fact that we are only on one side of the dialogue and cannot control the other side. Ippolit Terentyev wants to commit suicide in Dostoyevsky's novel *The Idiot* because he had no freedom in his own creation, but wants to assert his freedom in his destruction. In the character of Kirilov in Dostoyevsky's *The Devils*, this posture is elevated to that of the "man-god" who proposes to liberate all mankind from the fear of death through his own suicide. Stavrogin's suicide in *The Devils* is also a Modern Promethean assertion of willfulness in the face of his inability to discover the genuine will that plays its part in the dialogue of being and being, without trying to control and manipulate existence itself. Meursault is really a willful suicide of this sort in Camus's novel *The Stranger*, and Camus's Caligula (the hero of the play of that name), who makes of death the logical conclusion of the absurdity of a world in which men are unhappy and die, is, as Camus himself says, "a superior suicide."

The person who most clearly combines the heroic attitudinizing of the Modern Promethean with the "life of suicide" is Captain Ahab of Melville's *Moby Dick*—the man who identifies himself with a Truth which has no confines, the man who sees his path as laid on iron rails, the man who feels he must destroy the White Whale or be destroyed himself, and who destroys his ship, his crew, and himself in the process. "O lonely death on lonely life," Ahab cries out at the end. "O now I feel my topmost greatness in my topmost grief!"

Ignoring the absurd, underlining it, heroically revolting against it, or willfully defying it through "the life of suicide" does not exhaust the alternatives of the response of modern man to death. There is also that stance which I have designated in *Problematic Rebel, To Deny Our Nothingness,* and in this present book as trusting and contending, affirming in the midst of withstanding—a stance in which meaning is found in immediacy without any pretense to an overall, comprehensive meaning that would make the absurd anything less than absurd.

The first aspect of this stance is the recognition and acceptance of death. Death, Freud points out, is a debt we owe to nature. This does not mean the aesthetic, decadent welcoming of death of Swinburne's "Garden of Proserpine":

> From too much love of living
> From hope and fear set free,
> We thank with brief thanksgiving
> Whatever gods may be
> That no life lives forever,
> That dead men rise up never,
> That even the weariest river
> Winds somewhere safe to sea.

202

To a poem such as this, one can properly apply the strictures of Nietzsche's Zarathustra against the "preachers of death" who want to get beyond life in one "weary death-leap." Nor is this stance that of T. S. Eliot's Thomas à Becket, eager for martyrdom as part of a divine plan that will give him his place in the heavenly hierarchy.

It is perhaps that of Jesus in the Garden of Gethsemane saying, "Father, if it be Thy will may this cup be taken from me. Nonetheless, Thy will be done, not mine." It is clearly the stance of the twentieth-century American poet Theodore Roethke, who spent many of his later years in mental hospitals, picking himself up again after each blow that knocked his breath out and disoriented his mind:

> In a dark time, the eye begins to see,
> I meet my shadow in the deepening shade;
> I hear my echo in the echoing wood—
> A lord of nature weeping to a tree.
> I live between the heron and the wren,
> Beasts of the hill and serpents of the den.//
> What's madness but nobility of soul
> At odds with circumstance? The day's on fire!
> I know the purity of pure despair,
> My shadow pinned against a sweating wall.
> That place among the rocks—is it a cave,
> Or winding path? The edge is what I have.//
> A steady storm of correspondences!
> A night flowing with birds, a ragged moon,
> And in broad day the midnight came again!
> A man goes far to find out what he is—
> Death of the self in a long, tearless night,
> All natural shapes blazing unnatural light.[14]

There is no slightest admixture of acquiescence or surrender in this stance of the "Modern Job" vis-à-vis absurd death. "If there is a God," says Dr. Rieux in *The Plague,* "I should think as he sits above in silence, he would want us to fight the order of death." If "the plague" teaches that there is more to admire in men than despise, it is because of the courage to address and respond, not *in spite of* death and the absurd, but precisely to and including them. In his novels, Elie Wiesel shows us how a person who has lived through Auschwitz and Buchenwald can once again, finally, live in the present—bringing with him into that present all of the dead for whom he mourns. This is an unromantic posture, a fight for life without heroics, but it is also the only true courage—the only courage that is equal to life itself.

It is this courage that I find in Dylan Thomas's poem on his thirty-fifth birthday:

> Oh, let me midlife mourn by the shrined
> > And druid herons' vows
> The voyage to ruin I must run, . . .
> > . . . the closer I move
> To death, one man through his sundered hulks,
> > The louder the sun blooms
> And the tusked, ramshackling sea exults;
> > And every wave of the way
> And gale I tackle, the whole world then,
> > With more triumphant faith
> Than ever was since the world was said,
> > Spins its morning of praise. . . . [15]

I also find this courage in Annie Dillard. She proclaims that "evolution loves death more than it loves you or me" and that "we value the individual supremely, and nature values him not a whit."

She can also face her own death in a graphic way such as few would care to face it and find exultation in it:

> I am a sacrifice bound with cords to the horns of the world's rock altar, waiting for worms. I take a deep breath. I open my eyes. Looking, I see there are worms in the horns of the altar like live maggots in amber, there are shells of worms in the rock and moths flapping at my eyes. A wind from no place rises. A sense of the real exults me; the cords loose; I walk on my way.[16]

Dillard sees the dying praying at the last not "please," but "thank you," even people falling from airplanes. She finds meaning in the Dialogue with the Absurd:

> Divinity is not playful. The universe was not made in jest but in solemn incomprehensible earnest. By a power that is unfathomably secret, and holy, and fleet. There is nothing to be done about it, but ignore it, or see. And then you walk fearlessly, eating what you must, growing wherever you can, like the monk on the road who knows precisely how vulnerable he is, who takes no comfort among death-forgetting men, and who carries his vision of vastness and might around in his tunic like a live coal which neither burns nor warms him, but with which he will not part.[17]

The memory of death and the anticipation of death is often a calling to account, as in Kafka's novel *The Trial* and Tolstoy's *The Death of Ivan Ilyich*. "This door is meant for you, and now I am going to close it," says the doorkeeper to the dying man in Kafka's "Parable of the Law." We are called to account for the uniqueness of our lives and of the lives of all those with whom we have been intertwined—not in some Last Judgment or moralistic, idealistic, superego standard, but in the simple perspective of that moment when life and death are simultaneously present. "Why is man afraid of dying?" asked the Hasidic rabbi of Ger, and answered, "What man fears is the moment he will survey from the other world everything he has experienced on this earth."

Franz Rosenzweig begins *The Star of Redemption* with the reality of the fear of death and ends it with the phrase, "Into Life." Death is not of the future at all, nor of the past: It is an inescapable reality of the present. It is inescapable because it colors our existence at its far horizons. Yet all we ever know is the present, and all we know in that present is life itself. In the Talmud we are told that we should regard each day as if it were the one before our last. A kindred attitude is embodied in T. S. Eliot's meditation on the *Bhagavad Gita* in *Four Quartets*:

> Here between the hither and the farther shore
> While time is withdrawn, consider the future
> And the past with an equal mind.
> At the moment which is not of action or inaction
> You can receive this: 'on whatever sphere of being
> The mind of a man may be intent
> At the time of death'—that is the one action
> (And the time of death is every moment)
> Which shall fructify in the lives of others:
> And do not think of the fruit of action.

When we live with the death of one who was close to us, we know that the mystery of his or her having existed as a person and being with us no longer cannot be plumbed. It is part of the paradox of personal existence itself, which has no secure or continuous duration in time yet does really exist again and again in moments of present reality. We tend most of the time to think of death as an objective event that we can understand through our categories. But when we truly walk in the valley of the shadow, the imminence of death tells us something that we have really known all along: that life is the only reality that is given to us, that this reality—and not some continuing entity or identity of a personal nature—is all that we actually know. We do not know life without our individual selves, but neither do we know our selves without life. We know death, to be sure, but we know it as death-in-life. Life is the reality in which we share while we are alive.

To say that we once did not exist and again shall not exist is not to make our existence itself nothing; for this would be to equate reality with immutability. When you are dead and your body cremated and the ashes scattered, where are *you*? asks a Zen mondo. This is a question that cannot be answered in objective terms; for it is I myself that ask it of myself and am impelled to respond. I cannot think away my own present existence any more than I can deny "the undeniable / Clamor of the bell of the last annunciation, the bone's prayer to Death its God." All I can do is hold the tension of these two existential realities and live in that tension. "In order really to live," said Rabbi Yitzhak, the zaddik of Vorki, "a man must give himself to death. But when he has done so, he discovers that he is not to die—but to live."

Hermeneutical Appendix

Toward a Poetics of Dialogue

After the eras in literary theory stretching from the New Criticism and Structuralism to Deconstructionism and post-Deconstructionism, the present situation of literary criticism is necessarily a pluralistic one. I know of no better approach to that situation than to take seriously literature as dialogue and to enter in all seriousness into dialogue with literature. The present pluralistic situation calls for a nonhierarchical egalitarian model for the relationship between the reader and the text and between different interpretations, even though, as Martin Buber, the philosopher of dialogue, stresses, the struggle for a "common logos" is not a team hitched to a wagon but a strenuous tug of war.[1]

The most fruitful approach to literature, in my opinion, is to take seriously the full address of literature to the reader as a whole human person and to discover in our meeting with it that image of authentic human existence that is implicit in the very style of most great literature. In its very particularity, the image of the human in literature gives us the wholeness of the human as more abstract disciplines cannot. Next to the lives of actual persons, literature comes closest to retaining the concrete uniqueness of individual human beings while at the same time enabling us to enter into a sufficiently close relationship with these human beings that they can speak to us as bearers of the human—as exemplifications of what it does and can mean to be a human being.

It is for this reason that I claim in *To Deny Our Nothingness* that literature is the real homeland of the image of the human. But I also point out that it is the dialogue between author and character and between character and reader that produces the image of the human:

> No novel can present an image of the human if its author merely stands in objective relation to his character; none can present such an image if the author merely identifies with his character in a subjective way that destroys the aesthetic and personal distance between author and character. It is the dialogue between author and character that produces the image of human; this image is never a direct expression of the author's view, but a genuine product of this dialogue.[2]

The image of Kurtz in Joseph Conrad's *Heart of Darkness* comes from Conrad's presentation of a dialogue, spoken and unspoken, between Marlowe and Kurtz. The image that is produced never takes on the fixed quality of a visual image, but retains the open, unfinished quality of living dialogue. The dialogue between author and character also makes possible a dialogue between character and reader—the personal response of the reader that is, in the end, the most important element of any character's becoming an image of the human for him. He does not take over this character as an image through some sort of visual impression, but through a personal, even, in a sense, reciprocal relationship with him. Conrad's readers, too, have engaged in a continuing dialogue with Kurtz and with Marlowe and with the spoken and unspoken dialogue between them.

Literature as dialogue then implies the meeting between the image of the human, or basic attitude, of the reader and that of the author. The life of dialogue, as Martin Buber points out in *I and Thou*, "teaches you to meet others and to hold your ground when you meet them." Applied to the dialogue with literature, this means the combination of faithfulness to literature in its concrete uniqueness and otherness, including the whole fullness of style and form, with response to that literature from the ground of one's own uniqueness, one's life, and one's situation. Reversing the emphasis, we can say that approaching literature in terms of the image of the human implies not only bringing ourselves to the dialogue but the most faithful possible listening to the implicit intention, the underlying attitude, the point of view of the work of literature. Since every work of literature, even a poem, is a frozen speaking in which the voice must be liberated from the objective form, a really faithful listening will make it impossible to reduce the work to a single, directly expressed point of view. From this it follows that it is not the symbol, myth, or metaphor, still less the theological concept or metaphysical idea, but the tension of points of view that discloses the true depth-dimension of a novel or a play. Even in a poem it would be mistaken simply to identify the explicit I of the poem with the I of the author. To take one example I discuss in *Problematic Rebel*:

> By going all the way with Ahab and at the same time turning back with Ishmael and by holding the tension of these two opposing points of view within the form of *Moby Dick* itself, Melville creates an artistic meaning and balance great enough to contain his question, great enough, too, not to attempt an

answer. Melville's point of view comprehends both Ishmael's point of view and Ahab's without being identical with either, or being a moderate balance between them.[3]

This approach helps us avoid some of the most common forms of the *mismeeting* between reading literature and interpreting it. The most frequent form that this mismeeting takes is that of reducing a literary work to specific categories outside it. The great quarrels among schools of literary interpretation are often quarrels about how best we can truncate a great work of literature which should speak to us as a whole into one or another separate aspect. This is all too often common to all the contending schools.

Whether in *Moby Dick*, for example, you say the harpoons are phallic symbols, or falling into the whale's head a return to the womb, or you deal with it as the "hero journey," or see the whole thing in Jungian terms as a descending into the archetypal unconscious and working through to the individuation of the self, what you tend to do is to reduce the actual novel to the set of meanings that you have brought to it and prevent *its* saying what it is. This also means reducing the dynamic moving event of what takes place between you and the book to something which can be put into a static category.

Precisely the same thing happens if you approach literature looking for illustrations of a given philosophy or theology. Once more you destroy the concreteness of your encounter with the literature and make it subservient to already fixed patterns of thought. When Queequeg's coffin comes up at the end of *Moby Dick*, it might be taken as a resurrection symbol, as Milton Percival did in his *A Reading of Moby Dick*, just as in Dostoyevsky's novel *Crime and Punishment* there is a whole symbolism of Lazarus risen from the dead. Yet you cannot properly go from the symbol to the meaning of the book unless that symbol has become dramatically real in the book itself as it has not in either *Moby Dick* or *Crime and Punishment*. All these approaches find the meaning of literature in the static symbol or concept and not in the concrete unique event and its dramatic, dynamic unfolding in time.

A similar distortion is introduced by those who reduce a work to a single point of view—*Moby Dick* as "Melville's quarrel with God" or *Billy Budd* as a Christ symbol—or who identify the author's conscious intention with the intention that is implicit in the book.

Dostoyevsky wrote a letter to his niece in which he said, "I want Prince Myshkin to be a Christ figure, a really good man, a Don Quixote." But the intention that becomes manifest in *The Idiot* is very different from this conscious intention. Prince Myshkin is not in the least like Christ. He does not say to the woman caught in adultery, "Go and sin no more," but seeks instead to marry her and destroys both her and himself in the process. When Dostoyevsky wrote Book V of *The Brothers Karamazov*—Ivan and the Grand Inquisitor—he described it in a letter as the real center of the book. But when he wrote Book VI, he said the same thing. We cannot regard Ivan as identical with the Grand Inquisitor. We have to take into account his thwarted relationship with Smerdyakov and the extent to which he was a semiconscious accomplice in his father's murder. Neither can we take Father Zossima as the answer to the questions so agonizingly raised by Ivan, despite Dostoyevsky's assertion that he is; for he is only the other half. Ivan has the alienation, Father Zossima the closeness to nature and the spirit, and there is nothing that unites the two.

It is equally inadmissible to reduce Kafka's novels to a single point of view, whether it be nihilism, the insurance bureaucracy, the anticipation of the totalitarian state, waiting for grace, or God seen through the wrong end of the telescope. In a religious play such as T. S. Eliot's *Murder in the Cathedral* we have to recognize that the Thomas à Becket whom Eliot presents in the first act as a complex modern man, tempted by motives of pride to be lowest on earth in order to be highest in heaven, cannot be dramatically squared with the predestined martyr, the "Blessèd Thomas," of the second act. The dramatic effectiveness of the play is vitiated by an intention that is not worked through.

Dialogue means real meeting with otherness in contrast to dialectic, which usually takes place as the unfolding of a single consciousness through contrasting "points of view." Walter Stein understands this when he sees the task of the dialogical critic as being set for him by the problematic but essential demand that he reach out, through the most adequate confrontation and self-exposure he can achieve, toward the visions of reality that confront him. What makes this dialogue a real meeting with otherness rather than a reading in of theological or metaphysical assumptions is that "readiness to confront ultimate questions" that enables the critic's judgment to emerge from his "innermost grasp of, and response to, the work in its complex uniqueness; so that it will be informed by his antecedently organized responses to life, and at the same time be found irreducible to any terms other than itself." Stein continues:

> The critic, if he is doing his job, cannot operate from the outside, with the help of a series of theological norms: if he does not sit down humbly in front of this poem or novel, prepared to perceive it first of all on its own terms, and allow his response to develop from the centre of his personality, he will have nothing relevant to contribute.

In judging great literature, he is himself judged in his fundamental convictions.[4]

214

Stein is setting forth here what I have called the "dialogue of touchstones" in which we bring not only ourselves but our own touchstones of reality to the meeting with literature and let the touchstones of reality of the author speak to us at such a depth that new touchstones of reality may emerge for us.[5] An example I still think of is that of a Radcliffe friend who joined the Young Communist party out of a moral obligation she felt toward Tom Joad, the hero of John Steinbeck's novel *The Grapes of Wrath*.

Robert Detweiler approaches a profound understanding of literature as dialogue in his envisaging of what a religious reading of contemporary fiction might be like:

> The most positive and productive result of the narrative experience is not in persuading readers to accept a particular interpretation—not in overpowering them with a superior reading—but rather in provoking a compassionate reaction of mutual care and concern. Literary language as a mode of knowing ought to expand into a mode of *trustful* interacting, in which the risk-taking is made to pay off . . . by creating a community of response.[6]

Detweiler calls for "a *communitas*" of readers who confess their need of a shared narrative and encourage the creation and interpretation of a literature that holds in useful tension the fact that we live at once both liminally and in conclusion. Such a *communitas* of readers would provide not only a place where we belong but a context and structure within which we can constantly plot our lives. The storytellers of such a *communitas* articulate personal and communal experience to tell us more than we know.[7]

Another dialogical approach to literature, in addition to those we have considered above, is that of the American literary critic and philosopher of speech Walter J. Ong. Ong recognizes, as more and more contemporary critics are doing, that the chronological approach to literature of the traditional literary and intellectual historian must be complemented by a synchronic approach which not only keeps in view the fact that the literature of the past is read in and from the standpoint of the present, but also accepts the way in which contemporary literature modifies our relationship to the literature of antiquity.[8]

Still more important, Ong sets the appreciation and interpretation of literature within the dialectic of objective and aural correlatives, of literature as "a well wrought urn" and of the jinnee within the urn that cannot be expelled. This jinnee is the personal voice that no amount of form criticism can permanently banish, the voice of the I addressing the Thou that breaks through even the thickest of masks and the most remote of objective forms to reestablish the reality of the word that is spoken and the word that is heard. "A literary work can never get itself entirely dissociated from this I-thou situation and the personal involvement which it implies. . . . Poetry is often involved and mysterious, but by its very existence within our ken it is destined to communicate."

Drawing upon the two basic movements of distancing and relating that Martin Buber describes in his philosophical anthropology, Ong asserts that the greater the remoteness between the voice of the writer which creates the poem and those who hear or read it, the more evocative the work becomes. "All communication," says Ong, "is an attempt to crash through . . . the barriers which bar the ultimate compenetration of the 'I' and the 'thou.'" Thus for Ong the voice in literature is already a summons to faith in the sense of "trust in" rather than in the sense of "belief that." Faith in the possibility of communication is faith in someone with whom we can communicate.

Our belief in a play or a poem is thus an invitation to the persons involved in composing it and presenting it to us either to

216

say something worth our while or to betray our trust in them as persons. It involves a kind of openness to them and to their meaning at all levels.[9]

This openness to meaning at all levels, suggested by Ong, implies an openness to being changed by our encounter with literature. That faith to which Ong points is really existential and inter-human trust. This interhuman trust, this readiness to be open and respond without any prior commitment to assent, accounts for the possibility of an image of the human coming alive for us in our meeting with literature as Coleridge's "willing suspension of disbelief" could never do. It is only this personal involvement combined with obedient listening and faithful response to the voice of the other that addresses us in the novel, poem, or play that enables us to take literature out of the brackets of the purely aesthetic or the merely didactic so that our own image of the human, or basic attitude, may enter into dialogue with the image of the human, or basic attitude, underlying the work that confronts us.

What I have said above about literature as dialogue and about the dialogue between author and character finds powerful resonance in the writings of the late Soviet literary theorist Mikhail Bakhtin. The chief characteristic of Dostoyevsky's novels, according to Bakhtin's seminal book *Problems of Dostoevsky's Poetics*, is "a plurality of independent and unmerged voices and consciousnesses, a genuine polyphony of fully valid voices." The consciousness of a character is not turned into an object but is given as *someone else's* consciousness. The word of the character about himself and his world is as fully weighted as that of the author. "It is not subordinated to the character's objectified image as merely one of his characteristics, nor does it serve as a mouthpiece for the author's voice."

This extraordinary independence of the character's voice alongside the author's and that of the other characters constitutes a fundamentally new novelistic genre—the polyphonic novel.[10] "Dostoevsky's novel is dialogic." Its wholeness is constructed from the interaction of several independent consciousnesses which do not become an object (Buber would say an "It") for other characters, but remain a Thou which cannot be absorbed into other consciousnesses. There are no nonparticipant third persons, either in the point of view of the author or that of the reader, who must be, like the author, a participant in the overall dialogue of the novel. There is no place here for a "monologically all-encompassing consciousness."

Thus in contrast to those who make of the isolated consciousness their "touchstone of reality," to use my phrase, in Dostoyevsky consciousness is always found in intense dialogic relationship with another consciousness. It is important not to mistake this for "a meeting of true minds," for such disembodied mental interaction really characterizes dialectic. Ivan Karamazov and Rubashov in Arthur Koestler's *Darkness at Noon* are excellent examples of this, as are the dialectical and intellectual conversations of Settembrini and Naptha in Thomas Mann's *Magic Mountain.*

Bakhtin attributes to Dostoyevsky precisely that encompassing awareness of the other side of the relationship without losing one's own that Martin Buber calls "inclusion": "Dostoevsky had the seeming capacity to *visualize directly someone else's psyche.*"[11] In contrast to both empathy and identification, inclusion, or "imagining the real," as Buber calls it, means a bold imaginative swinging "with the intensest stirring of one's being" into the life of the other so that one can, to some extent, concretely imagine what the other person is thinking, willing, and feeling. Inclusion, or imagining the real, does not mean at any point that one gives up the ground of one's own concreteness, ceases to see through one's own eyes, or loses one's own "touchstone of reality." In this respect, it is the complete opposite of empathy in the narrower and stricter sense. Neither empathy, in the strict sense, nor identification can really confirm another person, since true confirmation means precisely that *I* confirm *you* in your uniqueness and that I do it from the ground of my uniqueness as a really other person.[12]

We do not see Dostoyevsky's hero but hear him, for he is not an objectified image but a *pure voice*. Only he can reveal himself in a free act of self-conscious discourse, for he can only be revealed as a Thou and not in the externalizing secondhand definition of an It.[13] Dostoyevsky's discourse about his characters is about *someone actually present* who hears the author and is capable of answering him.

Thus the new artistic position of the author with regard to the hero in Dostoyevsky's polyphonic novel is a fully realized and thoroughly consistent dialogic position, one that affirms the independence, internal freedom, unfinalizability, and indeterminacy of the hero.

> For the author the hero is not "he" and not "I" but a fully valid "thou," that is another and other autonomous "I" ("thou art"). The hero is the subject of a deeply serious, *real* dialogic mode of address. . . . And this . . . "great dialogue" of the novel as a whole takes place not in the past, but right now, that is, in the *real present* of the creative process.[14]

It is not surprising that Bakhtin uses Buber's terminology and shares his emphasis on the pastness of I-It and the presentness of I-Thou; for Bakhtin was deeply influenced by Buber. In an interview quoted in the *New York Review of Books* Bakhtin said that he thought of Buber as "the greatest philosopher of the twentieth century, and perhaps in this philosophically puny century, perhaps the sole philosopher on the scene."

Bakhtin then went on to explain that while Nicholas Berdyaev, Lev Shestov, and Jean-Paul Sartre are all excellent examples of thinkers, there is a difference between them and philosophers. "But Buber is a philosopher. And I am very much indebted to him. In particular for the idea of dialogue. Of course, this is obvious to anyone who reads Buber."[15]

Bakhtin also shares Buber's emphasis upon the alternation of distancing and entering relation as the heart of genuine dialogue:

> The author speaks not *about* a character, but *with* him . . . as another point of view. Only through such an inner dialogic orientation can my discourse find itself in intimate contact with someone else's discourse, and yet at the same time not fuse with it, not swallow it up, not dissolve in itself the other's power to mean . . . To preserve distance in the presence of an intense semantic bond is no simple matter. But distance is an integral part of the author's design, for it alone guarantees genuine objectivity in the representation of a character.[16]

Even the ideas that Dostoyevsky presents in his characters are part not of an authorial surplus of meaning but of the profound dialogic nature of human thought. So far from lying in one person's isolated, individual consciousness, as Descartes imagined with his *cogito ergo sum*, the idea begins to live and human thought becomes genuine only when it enters into genuine dialogical relationship with the ideas of *others*, ideas embodied in someone else's voice. The idea does not reside in a person's head but in dialogic communion *between* consciousnesses. Therefore, it "is a *live event*, played out at the point of dialogic meeting" and, like the word with which it is dialogically united, wants to be heard, understood, and "answered" by other voices.[17]

Having discussed Paul Celan's poetry in the final chapter of this book, we shall not be surprised that he also espoused fully consciously and intensely a "Poetics of Dialogue." Celan not only

220

conceives of language as being essentially dialogical, but, like Buber, views the poem as leading to the encounter with an essentially other reality embodied in the Thou. For Celan and Buber both all art is dialogical. Moreover, poetry creates a new reality by addressing "an addressable Thou." For both men finding and engaging a Thou in dialogue is indispensable for human existence.[18] For Celan, indeed, it was a *cri de coeur.* As James Lyon has pointed out, practically every one of Celan's poems, both in its content and its structure, is an attempted dialogue which tries to establish a link with existence. Every poem has explicitly and often repeatedly the Thou, even though, with the exception of his close friend Nellie Sachs, the German Jewish poet who lived in Sweden and shared his response to the Holocaust, we mostly do not know who the Thou is: "the woman addressed in a love poem or an alter ego or a deity or only the amorphous, unknowable 'other' to whom all Celan's poems make their way."[19]

In addition to this explicit Thou, Celan also saw his reader as a Thou and hoped, demanded, and expected that his reader would enter into dialogue with his poems. Thus Michael Hamburger asserts: "Such poetry demands a special kind of attention and perhaps a special kind of faith in the authenticity of what it enacts." "Attention is the natural prayer of the soul," Celan himself quotes Malebranche. "Celan's characteristic procedures . . . rest on an extraordinary trust in his readers' capacity to respond to the dominant gesture of a poem without access to the circumstantial data," writes Hamburger.[20]

The extent to which Celan uses Buber's language and strives to meet what Buber calls "the eternal Thou" is astonishing: *Gegenüber* (partner, one who is face to face), to which the poem addresses itself, the poem as a *Gespräch* (dialogue) with the "other" sphere, a *Begegnung* (meeting) with it. It is through this dialogue that the presence of the other can be evoked in the poem, as Celan himself states: "Into this presence its otherness is also brought with it by the addressed, which through being named has become a Thou."[21]

Celan "considered his poems not just as a vehicle with which to describe encounters with a '*Du*' but also as being instrumental in bringing them about," writes Robert Foot. "The core of the poem is the '*Du*' itself which is experienced as an almost tactile entity."[22]

The true poem cannot be paraphrased, as Buber points out. It would be a mistake to regard Celan's poems as embodiments of detached ideas or Dostoyevsky's novels as "novels of ideas," as has been so often done. Dostoyevsky did not think up ideas the way philosophers do. He *heard* them as they entered reality itself, including the "latent, unuttered future word," as "The Legend of the Grand Inquisitor" in *The Brothers Karamazov* so marvelously exemplifies. "Dostoevsky possessed an extraordinary gift for hearing the dialogue of his epoch," writes Bakhtin,

> or, more precisely, for hearing his epoch as a great dialogue, for detecting in it not only individual voices, but precisely and predominantly the *dialogic relationship* among voices, their dialogic *interaction*.[23]

In a telling comment on *Crime and Punishment* Bakhtin points out that the conventionally monologic epilogue cannot destroy "the powerful artistic logic of the polyphonic novel. Dostoyevsky the artist always triumphs over Dostoyevsky the journalist." Indeed, according to Bakhtin, Dostoyevsky thought not in thoughts but in voices, formulating each thought in such a way that a whole person sounded forth in it. Once in the margin of his manuscript of *Crime and Punishment* Dostoyevsky wrote next to a statement of Raskolnikov's, "Devil take it, he is right!" All of Raskolnikov's ideas, even those he publishes, are expressions of his whole person in its particular situation rather than abstract ideas valid by themselves. As a result of his embodiment of ideas in voices, in Dostoyevsky's novels, in contrast to the novels of Tolstoy, Turgenev, and Balzac, "there are absolutely no *separate* thoughts, propositions or formulations such as maxims, sayings, aphorisms which, when removed from their context and detached from their voice, would retain their semantic meaning in an impersonal form."[24] "All happy families are the same, each unhappy family is different," writes Tolstoy in the opening sentence of his novel *Anna Karenina*—an excellent example of an aphorism which is equally valid detached from its context.

Not only is the idea inseparable from the person, but also the voice of the person is inseparable from the dialogue between I and Thou. The "logic" of Dostoyevsky's ideas is dialogical. Indeed, what became explicit in the philosophy of Martin Buber two generations later was already implicit in the thought of Dostoyevsky as Bakhtin expounds it. Dostoyevsky's dialogical logic is in turn based upon a dialogical anthropology and a dialogical ontology: "A single person, remaining alone with himself, cannot make ends meet even in the deepest and most intimate spheres of his own spiritual life, he cannot manage without *another* consciousness. One person can never find complete fullness in himself alone." The reason for this is that personality means neither Descartes's solipsistic I nor an object but *another subject*: "The depiction of personality requires . . . *addressivity* to a *thou*."[25]

> A character's self-consciousness in Dostoevsky is thoroughly dialogized: in its every aspect it is turned outward, intensely addressing itself, another, a third person. Outside this living addressivity toward itself and toward the other it does not exist, even for itself. In this sense it could be said that the person in Dostoyevsky is the *subject of an address*. One cannot talk about

223

him; one can only address oneself to him. Those "depths of the human soul," whose representation Dostoyevsky considered the main task of his realism "in a higher sense," are revealed only in an intense act of address . . . at the center of Dostoyevsky's artistic world must lie dialogue, and dialogue not as a means but as an end in itself . . . in dialogue a person not only shows himself outwardly, but he becomes for the first time that which he is . . . not only for others but for himself as well. To be means to communicate dialogically. . . . Two voices is the minimum for life, the minimum for existence. . . .

The basic scheme for dialogue in Dostoyevsky is very simple: the opposition of one person to another person as the opposition of "I" to "the other."[26]

To be, for Bakhtin, too, means *to communicate.* The person does not dwell within himself but on the boundary; for his self-consciousness is constituted by his relationship to a *thou.* The loss of the self comes from separation, dissociation, and enclosure within the self. Absolute death is the state of being unheard, unrecognized, unremembered. Martin Buber says in strikingly similar fashion that abandonment is a foretaste of death, and abandonment is not just being left alone but being unheard as the unique person that one is, being "unconfirmed." Confirmation, as we have seen above, depends upon one person's concretely imagining what is really happening to and in the other.

In his study of Dostoyevsky Bakhtin finds that both the achievement of self-consciousness and the most important human acts arise out of the relation to a "thou." "Life is dialogical by its very nature. To live means to engage in dialogue, to question, to listen, to answer, to agree." In exact parallel to Buber's contrast between I-Thou and I-It, dialogue and monologue, Bakhtin defines "monologism" as the denial of the existence outside oneself of "another *I* with equal rights

224

(*thou*)." Authentic human life can only be verbally expressed in "*open-ended dialogue*" in which one participates wholly and throughout one's whole life. Entering into dialogue with an integral voice, the person "participates in it not only with his thoughts, but with his fate and with his entire individuality."[27]

Like Buber in his essay by that title in *The Knowledge of Man*, Bakhtin finds the significance of language in "the word that is spoken." In Dostoyevsky's world and in Bakhtin's too there are no objects or things but only subjects, no secondhand referential words but "only the word as address, the word dialogically contacting another word, a word about a word addressed to a word."[28]

> The word, the living word, inseparably linked with dialogic communion, by its very nature wants to be heard and answered. By its very dialogic nature it presupposes an ultimate dialogic instancing. To receive the word, to be heard. The impermissibility of *second-hand* resolution. My word remains in the continuing dialogue, where it will be heard, answered and reinterpreted.[29]

For Bakhtin the person departs, having spoken his word, but the word itself remains in the open-ended dialogue. The authentic sphere where language lives is dialogic interaction. "The entire life of language, in any area of its use (in everyday life, in business, scholarship, art, and so forth), is permeated with dialogic relationships. A dialogic reaction personifies every utterance to which it responds."[30]

To Buber, however, it is poetry even more than the novel that witnesses to the "word that is spoken":

> Were there no more genuine dialogue, there would also be no more poetry. . . . [The present continuance of language] wins its

life ever anew in true relation, in the spokenness of the word. Genuine dialogue witnesses to it, and poetry witnesses to it. For the poem is spokenness, spokenness to the Thou, wherever this partner might be. ... Poetry ... imparts to us a truth which cannot come to words in any other manner than just in this one, in the manner of this form. Therefore, every paraphrase of a poem robs it of its truth.[31]

If one follows this approach, then in the thought of Dostoyevsky and Bakhtin dialogue and the image of the human[32] converge "in a world of consciousnesses mutually illuminating one another." Even Christ, the highest and most authoritative voice, or image, for Dostoyevsky, crowns the world of voices, organizing but not subduing it.

Precisely the image of a human being and his voice, a voice not the author's own, was the ultimate artistic criterion for Dostoevsky: a fidelity to the authoritative image of a human being ... as something that stands *outside and alongside* and with which the author can enter into dialogic relations ... living beings who are independent of himself and with whom he is on equal terms.[33]

Dostoyevsky's creative stance, Bakhtin points out, does not imply that in him all positions are equally valid, as if the author passively surrendered his own viewpoint and truth.

Rather it is a case of an entirely new and specific interrelation between his truth and the truth of someone else. The author is profoundly *active*, but his action takes on a specific *dialogic* character. ... Dostoevsky frequently interrupts the other's voice but he does not cover it up, he never finishes it from the "self," that is from an alien consciousness (his own).[34]

In his philosophical anthropology, Buber distinguishes between "empathy," which goes over to the side of the other while giving up one's own, and "inclusion," which simultaneously imagine's the other while holding one's own ground. In closely similar fashion, Bakhtin distinguishes in *every* creative act between a first stage of empathy or identification and a reverse movement whereby the novelist returns to his own position. "Aesthetic activity begins properly only when one returns within oneself at one's place, outside of the one suffering, and when one gives form and completion to the material of identification." In close consonance with this Bakhtin sees "all events that are creatively productive, innovative, unique and irreversible" as presupposing the relationship of two consciousnesses that do not fuse.[35]

One of the most important aspects of the Poetics of Dialogue is the dialogue between text and reader. This dialogue is brilliantly illuminated for us by Steven Kepnes, to whom we owe the bold attempt to construct a "Buberian dialogical hermeneutic" and to bring it into connection with the major hermeneutic theorists of our time, including Bakhtin. What Kepnes says of the biblical text in his discussion of Buber's biblical hermeneutics is true of the dialogue between the reader and every real text: "The frozen script, in order to release its message, must be rescued from the written word and returned to the spoken through dialogue."[36]

The "word," the *logos* as used by Plato, Philo, and John, possesses eternal being whereas Heraclitus' still earlier use of the Greek *logos* of "speech-with-meaning," as Buber interprets it, is dynamic. This dynamism is also found in the Hebrew "Word" (*davar*) where it is connected to divine and human speaking. Biblical humanism does not see language as form and formation but as "an event in mutuality," says Kepnes paraphrasing Buber:

The biblical word arises out of concrete situations and events. It is fundamentally different from the word of the Greeks, which is "removed from the block of actual spokenness, sculpted with the artful chisel of thought, rhetoric, and poetry . . . [and] valid only when it becomes pure form."[37]

Buber insists that "the mystery of the coming-to-be of language and that of the coming-to-be of man are one." "There is no 'word' that is not spoken; the only being of a word resides in its being spoken."[38] "Buber does not find 'the house of being' in language [Heidegger]," comments Kepnes, "but, instead, designates the human being as the essential dwelling place of language." Kepnes also contrasts Buber with those poststructuralist theorists like Jacques Derrida who present language as a closed, self-referential system which can be analyzed separately from human speakers and from external references to the world.[39]

"Every attempt to understand the present continuance of a language as accessible detached from the context of its actual speakers, must lead us astray," writes Buber in "The Word That Is Spoken." It is from the spoken word, from human dialogue, that language draws its ontological power. Language derives from and contributes to the sphere of "the between," the I-Thou relationship. Language is a "system of tensions" deriving from the fruitful ambiguity of the word in its different uses by different speakers. In "The Word That Is Spoken" Buber finds the struggle for shared meaning essential to humanity: "It is the communal nature of the logos as at once 'word' and 'meaning' which makes man man, and it is this which proclaims itself from of old in the communalizing of the spoken word that again and again comes into being." In all these respects, as Kepnes points out, Buber is like Bakhtin.

The written word is never, for Buber, just a monument to past dialogue. It calls out for dialogue with the other, the Thou to whom it is spoken. In responding to the address of the literary work, the reader and interpreter lifts the written words anew "into the sphere of the living word" as a result of which the literary work "wins its life ever anew." This means no merging of I and Thou in the "fusion of horizons" that Gadamer anticipates, but a radical distinction between "I" and "Thou," that distancing which both Buber and Bakhtin see as essential to relation. It also does not mean staying enclosed within the dialogue between reader and text, but bringing one's interpretation into dialogue with others in that "common logos" and "communal speaking" which Buber points to in "What Is Common to All" (*The Knowledge of Man*).

In "The Word That Is Spoken" Buber makes a statement about the relationship between poetry, dialogue, and truth that complements while going beyond what Bakhtin has said about Dostoyevsky's truth. Buber distinguishes between faithful truth in relation to the reality that was once perceived and is now expressed, in relation to the person who is addressed and whom the speaker makes present to himself, and in relation to the factual existence of the speaker in all its hidden structure. This human truth opens itself to one in one's existence as this concrete person who answers with faithfulness for the word that is spoken by one.[40]

In contrast to the deconstructionist's total unconcern for the author, Kepnes' Buberian dialogical hermeneutic reestablishes the importance of the author "as the figure out of whose dialogue with other human beings and with language the work was produced." The figure of the author serves "as a warning never to cut the written text from the spoken word and the spoken word from the human being who speaks."[41] As Buber says, "the truth of language must prove itself in the person's existence."

Building on Buber's anthropological understanding of the "interhuman," the Bulgarian-French literary theorist Tzvetan Todorov joins Dostoyevsky and Bakhtin in stressing the I-Thou relationship between author and character and between reader and text. Surveying the vast and varied accomplishments of Bakhtin in the field of the human sciences, Todorov designates Bakhtin's all-encompassing theme as "the interhuman as constitutive of the human." Rather than putting forward an "architectonic of answer-ability" as do Clark and Holquist, Todorov sees Bakhtin's work as above all "heterology"—"plurality of voices remembering and anticipating the discourse that is past and to come," a "place of meetings." On this foundation Bakhtin, and Todorov following him, enunciate as the approach to literature a new "dialogical critique," hence that very approach to literature as dialogue and to the interpretative dialogue with literature that we have pointed to in this essay on the Poetics of Dialogue.

To accept this dialogical critique, says Todorov, means neither dogmatic absolutism nor relativism, but posing once again the question of truth. It means not considering truth as given in advance but seeking it as an ultimate horizon and regulative idea. Like Buber, Todorov recognizes that this is a truth that one can arrive at in the interhuman but not possess. Relativism and dogmatism exclude equally all authentic dialogue, Todorov quotes Bakhtin, in rendering it useless (relativism) or impossible (dogmatism). Dogmatism issues into a monological criticism, immanentism and relativism into the point of the view of the author studied, pure pluralism into a co-presence of voices which one analyzes immanently but which do not hear one another, says Todorov. "If one accepts the principle of common search of the truth, one will already be practicing dialogical criticism."[42]

Thus we have come full circle back to the theme with which we started this essay—the vital pluralism which is the necessary approach to literary criticism in our time, the dialogue between a reader whose self is constituted in dialogue and a text which is not limited either to author's intention or reader's interpolation, but

230

stands open to the ever new life and the ever new literary event of the moment. For this reason I would describe this vital pluralism as I have elsewhere described what I consider to be a realistic approach to modern faith—"a mutually confirming dialogue of touchstones."[43]

The only way we can escape the unfruitful alternatives of an essentialist and monolithic approach to self and text, on the one hand, and an empty relativism of self and text, on the other, is the dialogue with literature and the approach to literature as dialogue. The dialogical self stands in faithful dialogue with the text and the voice of the author and, just through this dialogue, with the other readers and interpreters of literature. Through their "tug of war" they build together the common "logos" of literature as "speech-with-meaning," enabling great literature to roll on from generation to generation "like a mighty stream."

Notes

Preface

1. Maurice Friedman, *Problematic Rebel: Melville, Dostoievsky, Kafka, Camus*, 2nd rev., expanded, and radically reorganized ed. (Chicago: University of Chicago Press, Phoenix Books, 1970).

2. Maurice Friedman, *To Deny Our Nothingness: Contemporary Images of Man*, 3rd rev. ed. with new preface and appendices (Chicago: University of Chicago Press, Phoenix Books, Midway Books, 1978).

Introduction: A Poetics of Meaning

1. Martin Buber, *Eclipse of God: Studies in the Relation between Religion and Philosophy*, introduction by Robert M. Seltzer (Atlantic

233

Highlands, N.J.: Humanities Press International, 1988), "Religion and Philosophy," trans. by Maurice Friedman, p. 35.

2. William James, *Essays in Pragmatism*, ed. with an introduction by Alburey Castell (New York: Hafner Publishing Co., 1949), p. 157.

3. Martin Buber, *A Believing Humanism: My Testament, 1902—1965*, trans. with Explanatory Comments by Maurice Friedman (Atlantic Highlands, N.J.: Humanities Press International, 1990), p 78 f.

Chapter 1—Mystics of the Particular

1. In his book *I and Tao: Martin Buber and Chuang-Tzu* (Albany: State University of New York Press, 1995), Jonathan Herman reports a scholar who has developed a typology of mystical insight or experience closely akin to my "mysticism of the particular": "Lee Yearley . . . introduces the new category of 'intraworldly mysticism,' which describes an aesthetically attuned and wholly earthbound state of being. What is so striking about the typology is that it posits a form of mysticism where 'no absolute reality is sought' beyond the inherent meaning of that which presents itself existentially; indeed, a mystic of this variety seeks nothing more (or less) than 'a way through the world.' " See Lee Yearley, "The Perfected Person in the Radical Chuang-tzu," in Victor H. Mair, ed., *Experimental Essays on Chuang–tzu* (Honolulu: University of Hawaii Press, 1983), pp. 125–139.

2. Witter Brynner, *The Way of Life According to Lao Tzu: An American Version* (New York: Capricorn Books, 1962), p. 37; *Tao Te Ching*, trans. with an introduction by D. C. Lau (Penguin Books, 1963), p. 78; *Lao Tzu, The Way of Life*, trans. by R. B. Blakney (New York: New American Library Mentor Books, 1955), p. 73; and Stephen Mitchell, *Tao Te Ching: A New English Version* with Foreword and Notes by Stephen Mitchell (New York: HarperCollins, Harper Perennial, 1991), Poem 21.

3. Bynner, *Way of Life*, p. 32; Lau, *Tao Te Ching*, p. 70; Blakney, *Lao Tzu*, p. 66; Mitchell, *Tao Te Ching*, Poem 14.

4. E. A. Burtt, ed., *The Teachings of the Compassionate Buddha* (New York: New American Library, Mentor Books, 1955), pp. 195–198.

5. Martin Buber, *Tales of the Hasidim: The Later Masters*, trans. by Olga Marx (New York: Schocken Books, 1961), p. 313: "The Way."

6. Ibid., p. 121: "The Teaching of the Soul," p. 286: "The Story of the Cape."

7. Ibid., p. 269: "What He Prayed With."

8. Thomas Traherne, *Centuries of Meditation*, ed. by Bertram Dobell (London: P. J. & A. D. Dobell, 1934), pp. 17–19.

9. William Blake, *Songs of Innocence and of Experience* with an introduction and commentary by Sir Geoffrey Keynes (New York: The Orion Press, 1967), plate 18.

10. Ibid., plate 37.

11. Ibid., plate 46.

12. T. C. McLuhan, *Touch the Earth: A Self-Portrait of Indian Existence* (New York: Simon & Schuster, Touchstone Books, 1971), p. 6.

13. Ibid.

14. Ibid., p. 36.

15. Walt Whitman, *Leaves of Grass: The First* (1855) *Edition*, ed. with an introduction by Malcolm Cowley (New York: Penguin Books, 1959), p. 27, vv. 42–45.

16. Ibid., p. 49, vv. 523–529.

17. Ibid., p. 55, vv. 662–665.

18. Ibid., p. 83, vv. 1271–1280.

19. Ibid., p. 85, vv. 1314–1316.

20. Ibid., p. 86, vv. 1329–1336.

21. Ibid., pp. 104, 113.

22. Ibid., p. 141.

23. Ibid., p. 145.

24. Fyodor Dostoyevsky, *The Brothers Karamazov*, trans. by Constance Garnett with an introduction by Marc Slonim (New York: The Modern Library, n.d.), book VI, chapter 3.

25. For a full-scale treatment of Heschel's thought see Maurice Friedman, *Abraham, Joshua Heschel and Elie Wiesel: "You Are My Witnesses"* (New York: Farrar, Straus & Giroux, 1987), part one, chapters 1–8.

Chapter 2—Poets of the Here and Now

1. B. J. Morse, "Rainer Maria Rilke and Martin Buber" in Irmgard Buck and George Kurt Schauer, eds., *Alles Lebendige meinet den Menschen. Gedenkbuch für Max Niehaus* (Bern: Francke Verlag, 1972), pp. 102–138. See also Maurice Friedman, *Martin Buber's Life and Work: The Early Years—1878–1923* (New York: E. P. Dutton, 1982; paperback edition, Detroit: Wayne State University Press, 1988), 412 f. note A to chapter 15.

2. Martin Buber, *The Legend of the Baal-Shem*, trans. by Maurice Friedman (New York: Schocken Books, 1977), p. 41.

3. Ibid., 47 f.

4. "But," comments Romano Guardini, "is it not strange that man shall accept the things and help them to the fullness of their being when it is said at the same time that he cannot be a home for other human beings, and love in the sense of the bond of I and Thou does not exist?" Romano Guardini, *Rainer Maria Rilkes Deutung des Dasein: Eine Interpretation der Duinesen Elegien* (Munich: Kösel-Verlag, 1953), p. 42, my translation. Romano Guardini summarizes Rilke's teaching in the *Duino Elegies*:

> There exist external things and human inwardness. But these two realms have a task in relation to each other. Man shall receive the things living into his soul, and thereby make them inward—the ninth elegy will say "invisible"—"transform" them. When he does that; when things become the content of life-experience (*Erlebnis*), only then do they in general gain their full being. But

conversely man shall also renounce bearing his inwardness only in himself. He shall give it to the world, and, to be sure, through an act of putting off the self (*Entselbstung*) through which he directs himself away from himself "into the open," out of his own isolation into the All . . . . When he does this, his inwardness becomes an element of external reality. The world takes on one more dimension; but he himself becomes liberated from the imprisonment in the I and becomes wholly what he should be. (Guardini, *Rilke's Deutung*, p. 38 f., my translation).

5. Rainer Maria Rilke, *Duino Elegies*. The German text, with an English translation, introduction, and commentary by J. B. Leishman and Stephen Spender (New York: W. W. Norton, 1939), p. 77.

6. Denise Levertov, *A Door in the Hive* (New York: New Directions, 1989), p. 43.

7. Denise Levertov, *Poems 1960–1967* (New York: New Directions, 1983), p. 17.

8. Ibid., p. 23.

9. Denise Levertov, *Oblique Prayers. New Poems and 14 Translations from Jean Joubert* (New York: New Directions, 1985), p. 76.

10. Ibid., p. 85.

11. Ibid., p. 86.

12. Ibid., p. 87.

13. Annie Dillard, *Pilgrim at Tinker Creek* (New York: Harper & Row, Perennial Library, 1985), pp. 8 f., p. 13.

14. Ibid., p. 76.

15. Ibid., pp. 80 f., 84.

16. Ibid., pp. 102 f.

17. Annie Dillard, *Teaching a Stone to Talk: Expeditions and Encounters* (New York: Harper & Row, Perennial Library, 1988), pp. 71 f.

18. Annie Dillard, *Pilgrim at Tinker Creek*, p. 251.

19. Annie Dillard, *Holy the Firm* (New York: Harper & Row, Perennial Library, 1988), p. 11.

20. Ibid., pp. 67 f.

21. Annie Dillard, *Teaching a Stone to Talk*, p. 138.

22. Wendell Berry, *Collected Poems: 1957–1982* (San Francisco: North Point Press, 1984), pp. 81, 86, 89, 94 f.

23. Ibid., p. 205.

24. Ibid., pp. 207 f.

25. Ibid., p. 240.

26. Ibid., p. 256.

27. Ibid., p. 263.

28. Wendell Berry, *Remembering: A Novel* (San Francisco: North Point Press, 1988), p. 122.

29. Ibid., pp. 123 f.

Chapter 3—The Shattering of Security

1. *The Collected Poems of W. B. Yeats*, definitive edition (New York: Macmillan, 1956), p. 184.

2. Chinua Achebe, *Things Fall Apart* (New York: Fawcett Crest, Ballantine Books, 1983), pp. 164 f.

3. Gustav Janouch, *Conversations with Kafka. Notes and Reminiscences* with an introduction by Max Brod, trans. by Goronwy Rees (London: Verschoyle; New York: Frederick A. Praeger, 1953), p. 50.

Chapter 4—Faith, Anguish, and Doubt

1. All page references are to the Modern Library edition of *The Brothers Karamazov*, trans. by Constance Garnett with an introduction by Marc Slonim (undated), p. 287.

2. Ibid., p. 289.

3. *The Complete Poems of Emily Dickinson*, ed. by Thomas H. Johnson (Boston: Little Brown & Co., undated), #185, #184, p. 87; #258, 118 f.

4. Ibid., #301, p. 142.

5. Ibid., #313, pp. 147 f.; #886, p. 420; #976, p. 456.

6. Ibid., #338, p. 160.

7. Ibid., #341, p. 162; #76, p. 179 f.; #377, p. 180.

8. Ibid., #476, pp. 229 f.

9. Ibid., #1413, p. 603.

10. Ibid., #1129, pp. 506 f.

11. *The Poems of Gerard Manley Hopkins*, 4th ed., rev. and enlarged, ed. by W. H. Gardner and N. H. MacKenzie (London: Oxford University Press, 1970), #33, p. 67; #37, pp. 69 f.

12. Ibid., #31, p. 66; #36, p. 69.

13. Ibid., #59, pp. 91–93.

14. Ibid., #61, pp. 97 f.

15. Ibid., #64, pp. 99 f.; #67, p. 101.

16. Ibid., #74, pp. 106 f.

17. Denise Levertov, *Candles in Babylon* (New York: New Directions, 1982), pp. 108–115.

18. Denise Levertov, *A Door in the Hive* (New York: New Directions, 1989), pp. 101–103.

19. Ibid., p. 64.

Chapter 5—The Demonism of Nature

1. For a full-scale interpretation see again the Melville section of Friedman, *Problematic Rebel: Melville, Dostoievsky, Kafka, Camus*.

Chapter 6—Human Demonism

1. *Black Elk Speaks. Being the Life Story of a Holy Man of the Oglala Sioux* as told through John G. Neihardt (Flaming Rainbow), illustrated by Standing Bear (New York: Washington Square Press, Pocket Books, 1972), pp. 166, 209.

2. Thomas Sanchez, *Rabbit Boss* (New York: Vintage Books, Vintage Contemporaries, 1989), pp. 522–525.

3. Ibid., p. 531.

4. Toni Morrison, *Beloved* (New York: NAL Plume Contemporary Fiction, 1988), p. 180.

5. Primo Levi, *Survival in Auschwitz: The Nazi Assault on Humanity*, trans. by Stuart Woolf (New York: Macmillan Collier Books, 1961), p. 22.

6. Ibid., p. 107. See Rollo May, Ernest Angel, and Henri F. Ellenberger, eds., *Existence: A New Dimension in Psychiatry and Psychology* (New York: Basic Books: 1958), pp. 132–138. "Each day life began anew, like a solitary island in a grey sea of passing time," p. 133.

7. Primo Levi, *Moments of Reprieve*, trans. by Ruth Feldman (Penguin Books, 1987), p. 172.

8. Primo Levi, *Collected Poems*, trans. by Ruth Feldman and Brian Swann (London, Boston: Faber & Faber, 1988), p. 65.

9. Primo Levi, *The Drowned and the Saved* (New York: Vintage Books, 1989), p. 60.

10. Ibid., p. 120.

11. See Maurice Friedman, *Abraham Joshua Heschel and Elie Wiesel: "You Are My Witnesses"* (New York: Farrar, Straus & Giroux, 1987), Part Two—"Elie Wiesel: the Job of Auschwitz."

Chapter 7—Kafka and Kundera:
Two Voices from Prague

1. See Maurice Friedman, *Problematic Rebel*, part IV, chaps. 13–17, pp. 285–410 and part VI, pp. 449–451, 475–491.

2. Milan Kundera, *Immortality*, trans. from the Czech by Peter Kussia (New York: Harper & Row, Harper Perennial, 1992), p. 11.

3. Ibid., p. 12.

4. Ibid., p. 248.

5. Ibid., p. 39.

6. Ibid., p. 40.

7. Ibid., p. 127.

8. Maurice Friedman, *The Human Way: Dialogical Approach to Religion and Human Experience* (Chambersburg, Pa: Anima Books, 1982), p. 79 f.

9. Kundera, *Immortality*, pp. 194 f.

10. Ibid., p. 200.

11. Aleene Friedman, *Treating Chronic Pain: The Healing Partnership* (New York: Plenum Publishing Co., Insight Books, 1992), chap. 20—"The Healing Partnership and the Common World." One of the theoretical bases of Friedman's integration of pain therapy and healing through meeting is her recognition that, more than any other experience, pain involves us in the unmaking of "the world"—in Martin Buber's sense of that common "cosmos" that we build together through our common "logos"—that common speech-with-meaning to which we contribute, each from our own unique place, in a strenuous "tug of war." Recognizing this, Aleene Friedman understands how it is the healing partnership alone that can bring the chronic pain sufferer back into the common world.

12. Kundera, *Immortality*, p. 258.

Chapter 8—The Harmonic, the Tragic, and the Grotesque

1. *The Collected Poems of W. B. Yeats*, definitive edition (New York: Macmillan Co., 1956), pp. 184 f.

2. Ibid., pp. 191 f.

3. Ibid., p. 246.

4. Ibid., pp. 292 f.

5. *Ibid.*, pp. 335 f.

6. *The Collected Poetry of W. H. Auden* (New York: Random House, 1945), pp. 50 f.

7. Ibid., p. 119.

8. *W. H. Auden: Selected Poems*, new edition, ed. by Edward Mendelsohn (New York: Vintage International, 1989), #13, p. 18.

9. *The Collected Poetry of W. H. Auden*, pp. 57–59.

10. Pablo Neruda, *Winter Garden*, trans. by William O'Daly (Port Townsend, Washington: Copper Canyon Press, 1986), pp. 7, 9.

11. Pablo Neruda, *Extravagaria*, a bilingual edition, trans. by Alastair Reid (New York: Farrar, Straus & Giroux, 1974), 49.

12. Pablo Neruda, *Fully Empowered*, trans. by Alastair Reid (New York: Farrar, Straus, & Giroux), pp. 133, 135.

13. Ibid., pp. 43, 45, 47.

14. Czeslaw Milosz, *Bells in Winter*, trans. by the author and Lillian Vallee (Manchesster, England: Carcanet New Press Ltd., 1982), pp. 7 f.

15. Ibid., p. 148.

16. Czeslaw Milosz, *Provinces*, trans. by the Author and Robert Hass (New York: The Ecco Press, 1991), p. 53.

17. Ibid., p. 55.

18. Ibid., p. 61.

19. Ibid., p. 66.

Chapter 9—The Scandal of the Particular

1. Yehuda Amichai, *Love Poems. A Bilingual Edition* (New York: Harper & Row, 1981), pp. 113, 115.

2. Yehuda Amichai, *Travels. A Bilingual Edition*, trans. from the Hebrew by Ruth Nevo (New York: The Sheep Meadow Press, 1986), p. 19.

3. Ibid., p. 15.

4. *The Selected Poetry of Yehuda Amichai*, ed. and newly trans. by Chana Bloch and Stephen Mitchell (New York: Harper & Row, 1986), p. 1.

5. Yehuda Amichai, *Amen*, with an introduction by Ted Hughes, trans. from the Hebrew by the author and Ted Hughes (New York: Harper & Row, 1977), p. 28.

6. Amichai, *The Selected Poetry*, p. 10.

7. Yehuda Amichai, *Time* (New York: Harper & Row, 1977), p. 13.

8. Amichai, *Amen*, p. 90; *The Selected Poetry*, p. 52.

9. Amichai, *The Selected Poetry*, p. 76.

10. Amichai, *Amen*, p. 69.

11. Amichai, *The Selected Poetry*, p. 138 f.

12. Ibid., p. 118.

13. Ibid., p. 138.

14. After Amichai's absurdist vision a positive statement is surely a Dialogue with the Absurd, since the Absurd itself does not go away or become anything less than Absurd. "Amichai's God is like no other God in Hebrew poetry," writes Glenda Abramson, "in that he represents the poet's own sense of need for universal order and his personal quest for meaning."(Glenda Abramson, *The Writing of Yehuda Amichai: A Thematic Approach* [Albany: State University of New York Press, 1989], p. 66.)

15. Amichai, *The Selected Poetry*, p. 126.

16. Amichai, *Amen*, p. 62.

17. Ibid., p. 66. "The poetry reveals that as the poetic 'I' grows older and less inclined to do battle with his spiritual deficiencies he submits to

the father and to God," writes Glenda Abramson in her thematic study of Amichai; but she also adds that God remains for Amichai "like a divine fossil, a reminder of the period of national faith," "an indictment not only of God's significance for man but also for his people, who have strayed so far from the covenant that he is preserved only as a monument to their spiritual history." Abramson, *The Writing of Yehuda Amichai*, p. 64.

18. Amichai, *Time*, p. 75.

19. Ibid., p. 31.

20. Amichai, *Travels*, p. 65.

21. Amichai, *Time*, pp. 54, 63.

22. "Amichai . . . is rescued from nihilism by statements of ideal and endeavor," writes Glenda Abramson, "expressed in richly textured language, recalling Camus' ability 'to grasp the edge of the cliff with his nails and hold on by God knows what miraculous instinct to survive.'" Abramson, *The Writing of Yehuda Amichai*, p. 78.

23. Amichai, *Time*, p. 26.

24. Amichai, *Travels*, p. 111.

25. Ibid., p. 127.

26. Denise Levertov, *Breathing the Water* (New York: New Directions, 1987), p. 81 f. (Original italics.)

27. Ibid., p. 83.

28. Denise Levertov, *A Door in the Hive* (New York: New Directions, 1989), p. 5.

29. Ibid., p. 38.

30. Ibid., p. 55.

31. Levertov, *Oblique Prayers*, p. 78.

32. Friedman, *To Deny Our Nothingness*, pp. 122–128.

33. Levertov, *Oblique Prayers*, pp. 82 f. (Original italics.)

34. Dillard, *Pilgrim at Tinker Creek*, pp. 7, 20.

35. Ibid., p. 146.

36. Dillard, *Holy the Firm*, pp. 45–48.

37. Ibid., p. 50.

38. Ibid., pp. 55 f.

39. Ibid., pp. 61 f., 70.

40. Dillard, *Teaching a Stone to Talk*, pp. 69–72.
41. Ibid., p. 151.
42. Ibid., p. 76.

Chapter 10—The *Shoah*—
Our Ultimate Confrontation

1. André Schwarz-Bart, *The Last of the Just*, trans. from the French by Stephen Becker (New York: Atheneum, 1973), p. 257.
2. Ibid., p. 267. (Original italics.)
3. Ibid., p. 284. (Original italics.)
4. Ibid., p. 309.
5. Ibid., p. 313.
6. Ibid., p. 324.
7. Ibid., p. 345 f.
8. Ibid., p. 374.
9. Martin Buber, *The Prophetic Faith*, trans. from the Hebrew by Carlyle Witton-Davies (New York: Macmillan Books, 1985), p. 234.
10. Martin Buber, *On Judaism*, ed. by Nahum N. Glatzer (New York: Schocken Books, 1967), p. 224 f. (Original italics.) Buber was dissatisfied with the original last paragraph of this English translation and asked me to retranslate it for him.
11. Levi, *The Drowned and the Saved*, p. 204.
12. Ferdinando Camon, *Conversations with Primo Levi*, trans. by John Shepley (Marlboro, Vt.: The Marlboro Press, 1989), p. 4. (Original italics.)
13. Maurice Friedman, *Religion and Psychology: A Dialogical Approach* (New York: Paragon House, 1992), pp. 119 f.
14. Levi, *Survival in Auschwitz*, p. 111.
15. Ibid., p. 113.
16. Ibid., p. 156.

17. Primo Levi, *The Reawakening*, "Afterword," trans. by Ruth Feldman (New York: Macmillan Collier Books, 1986), p. 215.

18. Ibid., p. 217.

19. Nelly Sachs, *O the Chimneys: Selected Poems, including the verse play ELI*, trans. from the German by Michael Hamburger, Christopher Holme, Ruth and Matthew Mead, and Michael Roloff, (New York: Farrar, Straus & Giroux, 1967), p. x.

20. Ibid., pp. 386 f.

21. Ibid., pp. 2 f. and 8 f. (The edition includes the German originals.)

22. Ibid., pp. 10 f., 16 f.

23. Ibid., p. 18 f.

24. Ibid., pp. 232 f., 244 f., 266–269.

25. *Poems of Paul Celan*, trans. and with an introduction by Michael Hamburger (London: Anvil Press Poetry, 1988), p. 63.

26. Ibid., p. 149.

27. Ibid., p. 283. See Hamburger's "Introduction," p. 27 f.

28. Katharine Washburn, "Introduction" to Paul Celan, *Last Poems. A Bilingual Edition*, trans. by Katharine Washburn and Margaret Guillemin (San Francisco: North Point Press, 1986), p. xxxv.

29. Hamburger, "Introduction" to *Poems of Paul Celan*, p. 22.

30. Ibid., p. 29.

31. *Poems of Paul Celan*, p. 153.

32. Ibid., p. 157.

33. John Felstiner, *Paul Celan: Poet, Survivor, Jew* (New Haven: Yale University Press, 1995), pp. 152, 156, 158.

34. Ibid., p. 169.

35. *Poems of Paul Celan*, p. 159; Felstiner, *Paul Celan*, p. 159.

36. Hamburger, "Introduction" to *Poems of Paul Celan*, p. 29.

37. Felstiner, *Paul Celan*, pp. 158, 199.

38. Ibid., pp. 153, 168 f.

39. *Poems of Paul Celan*, pp. 161, 175, 205.

40. I am indebted to the still unpublished criticism of the Celan scholar Dr. Heike Behl for this and a number of other insights into the relation between Celan and Jewish mysticism.

41. Ibid., pp. 227, 323.
42. Ibid., p. 325.
43. Ibid., pp. 331, 339.
44. Celan, *Last Poems*, pp. 100, 118, 133, 162, 174, 180.
45. John Felstiner, *Paul Celan: Poet, Survivor, Jew*, p. 278.
47. Ibid., p. 278.
48. Erich Kahler, cited in ibid., p. 247.

Conclusion—Confronting Death

1. W. C. Vanderwerth, *Indian Oratory: Famous Speeches by Noted Indian Chieftains*, foreword by William R. Carmack (Norman: University of Oklahoma Press, 1971), pp. 119–122.

2. Maurice Friedman, *A Dialogue with Hasidic Tales: Hallowing the Everyday* (New York: Human Sciences Press, 1988), p. 141. It is interesting here to note the Arapaho statement about the afterlife: "A man who dies fighting and a woman who dies in childbirth suffer the same fate. There is no difference in the afterlife of the good and the bad; all share the same world after death. It is the Arapaho way not to judge people" (Alice Marriott and Carol K. Rachlin, *American Indian Mythology* [New York: Thomas Y. Crowell Co., 1968], p. 195).

3. Margaret Craven, *I Heard the Owl Call My Name* (Toronto, Vancouver: Clarke, Irwin & Co., 1967), p. 12 f.

4. Buber, *Tales of the Hasidim: Later Masters*, p. 268: "The Meaning."

5. Martin Buber, *Daniel: Dialogues on Realization*, trans. with an introductory essay by Maurice Friedman (New York: Holt, Rinehart, & Winston, 1964), p. 130 f.

6. Rilke, *Duino Elegies*, Ninth Elegy, vv. 68–80, p. 77.

7. Bill McKibben, *The End of Nature* (New York: Random House, 1989).

8. T. S. Eliot, "The Dry Salvages," from *The Four Quartets*, from *Collected Poems 1909–1962* (New York: Harcourt Brace & World, 1971).

9. Robert Jay Lifton, *Death in Life: Survivors of Hiroshima* (New York: Random House, 1967), pp. 201, 480 f.

10. Ibid., p. 487. (Original italics.)

11. Ibid., pp. 490 f., 540 f. (italics mine).

12. Franz Rosenzweig, *The Star of Redemption*, trans. by William Hallo, with an Introduction by Nahum Glatzer (New York: Holt, Rinehart & Winston, 1971; New York: Schocken Books, 1972).

13. Martin Buber, *Between Man and Man*, trans. by Ronald Gregor Smith with an Introduction by Maurice Friedman (New York: Macmillan Books, 1985).

14. *The Collected Poems of Theodore Roethke* (Garden City, N.Y.: Anchor Press/Doubleday, 1975), "In a Dark Time," p. 231.

15. *The Poems of Dylan Thomas*, ed. with an introduction and notes by Daniel Jones (New York: New Directions, 1971), "Poem on His Birthday," pp. 208–211.

16. Dillard, *Pilgrim at Tinker Creek*, p. 242.

17. Ibid., p. 270.

Hermeneutical Appendix:
Toward a Poetics of Dialogue

1. Buber, *A Believing Humanism*, p. 46 f.

2. Friedman, *To Deny Our Nothingness*, p. 27.

3. Friedman, *Problematic Rebel*, p. 440 f.

4. Walter Stein, *Criticism as Dialogue* (London and New York: Cambridge University Press, 1969), pp. 12–16, 29, 31, 33 f., 42, 44.

5. See Chapter 1 of my book *Touchstones of Reality: Existential Trust and the Community of Peace* (New York: E. P. Dutton, 1972).

6. Robert Detweiler, *Breaking the Fall: Religious Readings of Contemporary Fiction* (San Francisco: Harper & Row, 1989), p. 27.

7. Ibid., p. 187.

8. Walter J. Ong, S.J., *In the Human Grain: Further Explorations of Contemporary Culture* (New York: The Macmillan Co., 1967), p. 37 f.

9. Walter J. Ong, S.J., *The Barbarian Within: And Other Fugitive Essays and Studies* (New York: The Macmillan Co., 1962), pp. 52 f., 55, 62, 65 f.

10. Mikhail Bakhtin, *Problems of Dostoevsky's Poetics*, ed. and trans. by Caryl Emerson, introduction by Wayne C. Booth, *Theory and History of Literature*, Vol. 8 (Minneapolis: University of Minnesota Press, 1984), p. 6 f.

11. Ibid., pp. 18, 36. (Original italics.)

12. Maurice Friedman, *The Healing Dialogue in Psychotherapy* (New York: Jason Aronson, 1985; paperback edition, Northvale, N.J.: Jason Aronson, 1994), chap. 17—"Empathy, Identification, Inclusion, and Intuition."

13. Bakhtin, *Problems of Dostoevsky's Poetics*, pp. 53, 58.

14. Ibid., p. 63. (Original italics.)

15. Mariya Kaganskaya, "Shutovskoi Khorovod," *Sintaksis* 12 (1984): p. 141. Quoted in Joseph Frank, "The Voices of Mikhail Bakhtin," *The New York Review of Books*, no. 16 (October 23, 1986): 56.

16. Bakhtin, *Problems of Dostoevsky's Poetics*, p. 63 f.

17. Ibid., p. 87 f.

18. James K. Lyon, "Paul Celan and Martin Buber: Poetry as Dialogue," *PMLA* 86 (1971): 111, 116 f., 119. "Gedichte . . . halten auf . . . eine ansprechbares Du vielleicht, auf eine ansprechbare Wirklichkeit" (Bremen speech, p. 11, quoted in Lyon, p. 111). "Das Gedicht ist einsam. Es ist einsam und unterwegs. Wer es schreibt, bleibt ihm mitgegeben. Aber steht das Gedicht nicht gerade dadurch, also schon hier, in der Begegnung—*im Geheimnis der Begegnung*? Das Gedicht will zu einem Andern, es braucht dieses Andere, es braucht ein Gegenüber. Es sucht es auf, es spricht sich ihm zu" (*Der Meridian Rede anlässlich der Verleihung des Georg Büchner Preises 1960* [Frankfurt/Main: S. Fischer,

1961], p. 18, quoted in Lyon, p. 119, n. 8). "Das Gedicht [ist] eine Erscheinungsform der Sprache und damit seinem Wesen nach dialogisch." Paul Celan, *Ausgewählte Gedichte*, p. 128, quoted in Lyon, p. 116. (Original italics.)

19. *Poems of Paul Celan*, Michael Hamburger, "Introduction," p. 30.

20. Ibid., p. 31 f.

21. Paul Celan, *Der Meridian Rede*, in Celan, *Ausgewählte Gedichte*, pp. 133–148, quoted in German in Foot (see next note), p. 207 f., my translation. It was only after I remarked in the text about the striking resemblance between Buber's terminology and Celan's that I came across James K. Lyon's "Paul Celan and Martin Buber: Poetry as Dialogue," *PMLA* 86 (1971): 110–20.

22. Robert Foot, *The Phenomenon of Speechlessness in the Poetry of Marie Luise Kaschnitz, Guenter Eich, Nelly Sachs and Paul Celan. Studien zur Germanistik, Anglistik und Komparatistik*, ed. by Armin Arnold and Alois M. Haas, Vol. 110 (Bonn, Germany: Bouvier Verlag Herbert Grundmann, 1982), pp. 216–218.

23. Bakhtin, *Problems of Dostoevsky's Poetics*, p. 90. (Original italics.)

24. Ibid., pp. 292, 93, 95.

25. Ibid., pp. 299, 99 f., 177, 300.

26. Ibid., p. 251 f. (Original italics.)

27. Ibid., p. 292 f.

28. Ibid., p. 237.

29. Ibid., p. 300. (Original italics.)

30. Ibid., p. 183 f.

31. Martin Buber, *The Knowledge of Man: A Philosophy of the Interhuman*, ed. with an introductory essay (chap. 1) by Maurice Friedman (Atlantic Highlands, N.J.: Humanities Press International, 1988), "The Word That Is Spoken," trans. by Maurice Friedman, pp. 101, 108.

32. To Dostoyevsky the image of the human is "not a finalized and closed image of reality (a type, a character, a temperament), but an open image-discourse," Bakhtin elucidates in a note (*Problems of Dostoyevsky's Poetics*).

33. Ibid., 97, 284. (Original italics.)

34. Bakhtin, *Problems of Dostoyevsky's Poetics*, quoted in Tzvetan Todorov, *Mikhail Bakhtin: The Dialogical Principle*, trans. by Wlad Godzich, *Theory and History of Literature*, Vol. 13 (Minneapolis: University of Minnesota Press, 1984), p. 106. (Original italics.)

35. Todorov, *Mikhail Bakhtin*, pp. 96 f., 99 f.

36. Steven Kepnes, *The Text as Thou: Martin Buber's Dialogical Hermeneutics and Theological Narrative* (Bloomington: Indiana University Press, 1992), p. 57.

37. Ibid., p. 59.

38. Buber, *Knowledge of Man*, "The Word That Is Spoken," trans. by Maurice Friedman.

39. Kepnes, *The Text as Thou*, p. 62.

40. Buber, *Knowledge of Man*, p. 110.

41. Kepnes, *The Text as Thou*, p. 75. Kepnes finds the structure of Buber's thought especially well-suited to narrative expression:

> The overall thrust away from philosophical concept to existential experience and encounters, the focus on individual characters and the transformation of character through event, the search for the moment of change from the ordinary to the extraordinary, the focus on human relationship, these central themes of the philosophy of I-Thou make narrative more than just a convenient technique for illustration. Buber's philosophy is concerned with inherently narrative themes. . . . Narrative, in its capacity to draw and reveal relationships between event and event, person and person, is peculiarly apt to reveal the dimension of "the between" which is so important to Buber. (Kepnes, pp. 86 f.)

The I-Thou event in the middle of Buber's own narratives functions to give order and meaning to the plot because it "breaks in upon and transforms the ordinary into the extraordinary, . . . passing time into significant time, . . . the persons involved into beings who are no longer the same as they were when they entered into relationship" (Kepnes, p. 100). A good example of this predominance of the middle is Buber's story of his mother in his autobiographical fragments. The true turning point of this story is not Buber's reflection at the end about genuine meeting, but the moment in the center when the little girl who is taking care of the four-year-old Buber answers his question about his mother with the words, "No, she will not come back." Kepnes comments:

> Buber's middle . . . is the focal point of the plot. It is in the middle that the "theme," the "point," of the story is to be found. . . . As the present moment is the time in which I-Thou events occur, . . . the middle represents the time when we are in direct contact with other humans. . . . Life transpires in the "between," . . . between birth and death. . . . For Buber, it is in this full moment that we are put in contact with our origins and with our future. . . . As Buber says in *I and Thou*: "For this finding is not the end, but only the eternal middle, of the way." (Kepnes, p. 97 f.)

Kepnes also asserts that Buber's narratives "present that mix of order and disorder, of illumination and doubt, of abiding question and surprise that is at the heart of the I-Thou encounter." The ambiguity of the story gives it its "hermeneutic potential," says Kepnes, opening "the window to the interpretive process which begins in reading and ends in the reader's own life meetings" (Kepnes, p. 102).

42. Tzvetan Todorov, *Critique de la critique: Un Roman d'apprentissage* (Paris: Éditions du Seuil, 1984), pp. 89 f., 96, 101–103, 187, 190 (my translation).

43. Maurice Friedman, *A Heart of Wisdom: Religion and Human Wholeness* (Albany: State University of New York Press, 1992).